TEXTS AND TRANSLATIONS 1

PSEUDEPIGRAPHA SERIES
1

PARALEIPOMENA JEREMIOU

Edited and Translated by
ROBERT A. KRAFT
and
ANN-ELIZABETH PURINTUN

SOCIETY OF BIBLICAL LITERATURE
1972

PARALEIPOMENA JEREMIOU

Copyright © 1972
by
The Society of Biblical Literature

All rights reserved. No part of this book may be reproduced or utilized in any form or by any means, electronic or mechanical, including photocopying, without permission in writing from the Publisher.

Library of Congress Catalog Card Number: 72-88436

PRINTED IN THE UNITED STATES OF AMERICA
PRINTING DEPARTMENT, UNIVERSITY OF MONTANA, MISSOULA, MONTANA 59801

PREFACE TO THE SERIES

TEXTS AND TRANSLATIONS is a project of the Committee on Research and Publications of the Society of Biblical Literature and is under the general editorial direction of Robert W. Funk (University of Montana), Hans Dieter Betz (School of Theology at Claremont), Robert A. Kraft (University of Pennsylvania), and George W. MacRae (Weston College). The purpose of the series is to make available in convenient and inexpensive format ancient texts which are not easily accessible but are of importance to scholars and students of "biblical literature" as broadly defined by the SBL. Reliable modern English translations will accompany the texts. Occasionally the series will include documents not published elsewhere. No effort is made in these publications to provide new critical texts, nor to furnish extensive annotations. The series is regarded as provisional, and individual volumes may be replaced in the future when better textual evidence is available.

For the "Pseudepigrapha Series" the choice of texts is governed in part by the research interests of the Pseudepigrapha Seminar of the SBL of which Walter Harrelson (Vanderbilt Divinity School) is Chairman and James H. Charlesworth (Duke University) Secretary. This series will regularly include volumes incorporating the fragmentary evidence of works attributed to biblical personalities, culled from a wide range of Jewish and Christian sources. The volumes are selected, prepared, and edited by the following subcommittee of the Pseudepigrapha Seminar:

    Robert A. Kraft (University of Pennsylvania)
    George W. MacRae (Weston College)
    George Nickelsburg (University of Iowa)
    Michael E. Stone (Hebrew University)
    John Strugnell (Harvard University)

INTRODUCTION

This slim volume is intended as a progress report and a stimulus to further work. The materials presented here are in every way "provisional." We have attempted to list the MSS of ParJer known to us, but we have not yet secured microfilms or reproductions of them all, nor have we been able even to check all of the published descriptions for each of the MSS as yet. Our work on the SHORT FORM of ParJer (= "men" in some of the notes to the translation) has only just begun, and we have barely scratched the surface of the problems presented by the Dorotheus SYNOPSIS material (= "hist" in the notes)—we understand that Professor Emilè Turdeanu has been working on certain aspects of the latter in France.

The English translation of ParJer first appeared in the 1971 SBL Seminar Papers. Its verse divisions differ slightly from older editions, and it is based on the Greek text which appears here for the first time. We have corrected errata in the translation, and have revised a few passages to agree more closely with the Greek text. Except for one or two passages, the critical notes have not been updated, although we have considerably more information in hand now than we did when the translation was prepared in 1971. For the most part, the apparatus still reflects accurately the sorts of differences that exist between the different textual groupings described below.

Numerous acknowledgements are in order. Only a few can be mentioned here. We especially appreciate the comments and assistance offered by members and friends of the PHILADELPHIA SEMINAR ON CHRISTIAN ORIGINS and the SBL PSEUDEPIGRAPHA SEMINAR, before whom some of these materials have been presented at various stages of development. And the many hands which assisted in the difficult task of typing these complicated materials deserve special mention. Finally, to Robert W. Funk for his pioneering part (both in terms of ideas and enthusiasm, and in actual physical labor) in making this type of publication a reality for American scholarship, our profound thanks!

Philadelphia   Ann-Elizabeth Purintun
July 1972   Robert A. Kraft

TEXTUAL WITNESSES

The eclectic Greek text of the LONG FORM of ParJer presented here is provisional in nature, based on the editors' examination of a portion of the preserved evidence. Ultimately we intend to examine all available witnesses. For the present, the following patterns of textual relationship have emerged:

The LONG FORM of ParJer is preserved in numerous Greek MSS (23 have been identified thus far) as well as in several versions. Sometimes this material is designated in the MSS to be read on 1 May. The witnesses may be subdivided into several groups:

BAH arm slav (+ ? F)

    B = Jerusalem Taphos (Sepulcher) 34, fol 251ff, 10/11 century (this MS was used by Harris in his 1889 edition).
    A = Milan Braidensis AF IX 31, fol 1-10, 15 century (published by A. M. Ceriani in 1868, and used by Harris in his 1889 edition).
    H = Oxford Bodleian Holkham gr 27, fol 292-303, 15 century.
   arm = Armenian version of the long form published by H. S. Josepheantz (Venice, 1896; pp. 349-377) and translated by J. Issaverdentz (Venice, 1901, 1907[2]; repr. of 1901 ed in 1934), from the late 15th century Etchmiadzin MS 920 (additional information on the arm material has been supplied by Michael Stone of the Hebrew University at Jerusalem).
  slav = Old Church Slavic version published by Tichonravov in Russian (Moscow, 1863) from a 16th century MS, and collated against the apparatus of the Harris edition by N. Bonwetsch (1891).
  (F = Florence Laurentiana plut IV cod 6, fol 232-249^r, 11 century, should probably be added to this group, judging from its published incipit and explicit.)

PO WS J : these five Greek MSS exhibit a text form sufficiently different from the other groupings to warrant separate treatment. Within this grouping, two identifiable sub-groups are to be found in PO and WS respectively.

    P = Paris gr 1534, fol 159-169, 11 century.
    O = Oxford Bodleian Barocc 240, fol 1^v-9, 12 century.
    W = Vienna Hist gr 126 (formerly 36), fol 39-48^r, 14 century (?).
    S = Sinai gr 1670, fol 116-130^r, 16 century.
    J = Jerusalem Saba 281, fol 118-125^r (old fol nos. 134-141), 13 century.

C eth (L) (+ ? I M) : Harris already noted the close relationship exhibited between his MS C and the eth version. Now the fragment from L lends sporadic but characteristic support to this group. (Judging from the published incipits of MSS IM, they also belong to this grouping.)

    C = Jerusalem Taphos (Sepulcher) 6, fol 242-247^r, 10 century. In the middle of ParJer 8.5 the text of C leaves ParJer and continues with other material—a prayer, narrative of return of exiles under Cyrus, rebuilding of temple, coming of Ezra—without any indication of a break. (The MS was used by Harris in his 1889 edition.)
   eth = Ethiopic version published on the basis of three MSS by A. Dillmann (1866) and translated into German independently by F. Prätorius (1872) and E. König (1877). There is also a French translation by R. Basset (1893). Currently, W. Baars of Leiden is assisting with the eth materials.

L = Leiden University Library Bibl. Gr 99, folio 119, 14 century. An isolated folio containing two full pages from ParJer 5.32b-7.36a. Along with a number of otherwise unattested readings, L contains some readings characteristic of the C eth text.

(I = Jerusalem Saba 373, fol 129-142 (?), 16 century. The final folio of our text is missing, according to the catalogue.)

(M = Venice St. Mark VII.45 (formerly Nanianus 161), fol 254-262, dated 1616-1618.)

Other known MSS of the LONG FORM are:

G = Athens 1027, fol 402-411, 12 century.
K = Athos Lavra 327 (formerly T 87), fol 159-168^r, 13 century.
N = Paris suppl gr 136, fol 107-134, 16 century.
R = Leningrad Bibl Publ 96, fol 78^v-89, 12 century.
T = Cambridge Trinity 191 (formerly B 8.7.58), fol 422-431, 11/12 century.
U = Vatican Palatine 27, fol 149-154, 10/11 century.
V = Vatican gr 620 (formerly 420), fol 201-206, 16 century.
X = Paris gr 760, fol 176^v-181, 14 century.
Y = Paris gr 776, fol 9-16, 15 century.
Z = Paris gr 1190, fol 186^v-196, dated 1568.

Note: in the index to MS gr 504, from the 10/11 century, ParJer is listed as item no. 12, but the actual text for items nos. 7-17 is lacking.

A SHORT FORM of ParJer is also preserved in numerous witnesses, including some 40 Greek MSS, two Armenian recensions, and also a Slavic version. Menologion/Synaxarion MSS frequently include the ParJer material under the date of 4 November, usually preceded by Jeremiah legends from the Lives of the Prophets, etc. In the MSS examined thus far, the general title given to this collection of Jeremiah traditions is NARRATIVE CONCERNING THE LAMENT OF THE PROPHET JEREMIAH CONCERNING JERUSALEM AND CONCERNING THE CAPTURE THEREOF AND CONCERNING THE ECSTATIC TRANCE OF ABIMELECH, with the following subtitle introducing the ParJer section proper: CONCERNING THE CAPTURE OF JERUSALEM WHICH THE LORD ANNOUNCED TO JEREMIAH.

A modern Greek version of this material is also included in the work attributed to Dorotheus of Monembasia entitled SYNOPSIS OF THE VARIOUS HISTORIES (1631), which has appeared in various somewhat different forms in Greek, and also in at least a Slavic and Rumanian version. This material is closely related to the SHORT FORM of ParJer, and is almost surely based on it, although the SYNOPSIS presents some interesting differences as well.

We have only begun to analyze this extensive and complicated material in any systematic fashion. Thus far, the following pattern is emerging:

eg a v (+ ? j l m p) : these Greek MSS seem to contain virtually the same text form of the SHORT RECENSION of ParJer. MSS e and g stand closest to each other, with a and v deviating a bit more from eg and from each other than e and g deviate among themselves. (Judging from titles and incipits published in the catalogues, MSS j, l, m, and p should also be included in this general grouping.)

TEXTUAL WITNESSES

- e = Jerusalem Stauros (Crucis) 35, fol 391ᵛi-395, 15 century (consulted occasionally by Harris for his 1889 edition).
- g = Sinai gr 529, fol 214-227 (old fol nos. 201-214), dated 1555.
- a = Jerusalem Saba 226, fol 227ii-230, 15/16 century.
- v = Vatican Barberini 3, fol 153-172, dated 1497 (published by Vassiliev in 1893; lacks ParJer 8.3b-9.14, possibly due to missing folio in archetype).
- (j = Athens 346, fol 42-50, 15 century.)
- (l = Athens 422, item 39, dated 1546.)
- m = Athos 2801 [= Dochiariou 127], item 21, 17 century.)
- (p = Athos 3797 [= Dionysios 263], item 23, 17 century.)

dh (+ ? o) : these Greek MSS agree in characteristic differences from the above grouping. (Judging from published catalogue information, MS o should also be included with dh.)

- d = Jerusalem Taphos 66, fol 208ᵛ-211 (old fol nos. 212-215), 15/16 century (used by Harris occasionally in his 1889 edition).
- h = Sinai gr 531, fol 61-72, 15/16 century.
- (o = Athos 3766 [= Dionysios 232], fol 530ᵛ-537 (item 16), 17 century.)

Other Greek MSS suspected of containing the SHORT FORM of ParJer are:

- b = Jerusalem Saba 429.II, item 7, dated 1619.
- c = Jerusalem Stauros 118, fol 52ᵛ-66ᵛ, 18 century.
- f = Alexandria Patriarchal Library 173, fol 88-113, 16 century.
- i = Andros 46, fol 203-210, 15 century.
- k = Athens 356, fol unknown, dated 1634.
- jj = Athens 838, item 9, 16 century.
- kk = Athens Amantos A, fol 86-93, date unknown.
- n = Athos 3695 [= Dionysios 161], item 6, 17 century (title: The Word of Jeremiah and Baruch and Abimelech that Jerusalem would be given over to Babylon, to the Hands of the Chaldeans [!]).
- mm = Athos Lavra Γ 87, fol unknown, date unknown.
- nn = Athos Lavra H 206, fol 115-118, 16 century.
- oo = Athos Lavra K 18, fol 157-169, 17 century.
- q = Ochrid (Yugoslavia) 29, fol 300-315, dated 1547.
- qq = Milan Ambrosian Library A.79 supp, fol unknown, 15 century (consulted by Ceriani and cited in his 1868 edition).
- r = Munich 255.1, fol 94-102, 15/16 century.
- rr = Munich 366, fol unknown, date unknown.
- s = Vatican gr 1190.114, fol 1044-1049, 16 century.
- t = Vatican gr 1192.7, fol 79-86, 15 century.
- u = Vatican gr 1700 (= Lollino 16), fol 114ff, date unknown.
- ss = Vatican Palatinae 138, fol 346-353, 14 century.
- tt = Vatican Reginae 49, fol 95ᵛ-102/103, dated 1574.
- vv = Vatican Barberini 284, fol unknown, date unknown.
- w = Paris gr 947, fol 297ᵛ-298 (only the beginning) dated 1574.
- x = Paris gr 1313, fol 325-329, 15 century.
- y = Paris gr 1579, fol 91-96, 15 century.
- ww = Paris gr 1582, fol 109ᵛ-114, 13/14 century.
- xx = Paris suppl gr 54, fol 89-94, 16 century.
- yy = Paris suppl gr 1036, fol 12ff(?), 16 century (fragmentary ?).
- z = London British Museum add 10073, fol 271ᵛ-281, 16 century.
- zz = London British Museum Harley 5782, fol unknown, 14 century.

ANNOTATED CHRONOLOGICAL BIBLIOGRAPHY

At this stage of our investigations of ParJer, we are not ready to make critical judgments regarding such matters as the original language, authorship, date, redactional strata, sources, etc. Instead, we offer the following survey of what others have written about ParJer, in hopes that it will help draw attention to some of the problem areas that have been identified. Ms. Purintun proposes to pursue such questions in her doctoral dissertation at the University of Pennsylvania.

1861   Ceriani, A. M.   MONUMENTA SACRA ET PROFANA 1.1 (Milan), xiii. Provides general information about ParJer (Greek MSS a and qq, eth, use of another MS by Wetstein on Mk 11.13, etc.), which is quoted by Ceriani in his 1868 edition.

1863   Tichonravov, N.   Two volume work in Russian on Slavic apocryphal literature (St. Petersburg), vol 1, 284-297. Russian translation of ParJer slav from a 16th century MS. Also SHORT FORM on pp. 273-284.

1866   Dillmann, A.   "Reliqua Verborum Baruchi," in his CHRESTOMATHIA AETHIOPICA (Leipzig), viii-x. ParJer is hesitatingly dated to the 3-4 centuries CE because of its affinities to Ascension of Isaiah [see also Dillmann's article on pseudepigrapha in the Herzog Realencyc.[2] 12 (1883), 358, where the Greek origin of ParJer is affirmed, and it is dated after Syriac Baruch and Asc Isa as a Christian haggadic work of the 3rd century or even later]. An edition of the Ethiopic text, with a Latin translation, are provided.

1867   Ewald, H.   Review of Ceriani's earlier volumes in GÖTTINGISCHE GELEHRTE ANZEIGEN, p. 1714. ParJer is called a Christian composition, and dated later than Syriac Baruch, on which it is said to be based [see also Ewald's discussion in his GESCHICHTE DER AUSGÄNGE DES VOLKES ISRAEL 7 (1868[2]), in his treatment of Elkesaite baptism].

1868   de Groot, P. H.   BASILIDES AM AUSGANGE DES APOSTOLISCHEN ZEITALTERS ALS ERSTER ZEUGE . . . (Leipzig), 94 n.1. Follows Dillmann regarding origin and date of ParJer, and claims that ParJer has nothing to do with the gnostic Baruch but does have affinities to Syriac Baruch.

1868   Ceriani, A. M.   "Paralipomena Jeremiae Prophetae," in his MONUMENTA SACRA ET PROFANA 5.1 (Milan), 9-10. Introduces his edition of Greek MS A by referring explicitly to the claims of Dillmann, Ewald, and de Groot (Ceriani denies any expertise in the study of apocrypha on his own part).

1871   Fritzsche, O. F.   LIBER APOCRYPHI VETERIS TESTAMENTI (Leipzig), xxxii. Dates ParJer later than Syriac Baruch (which in turn is dated soon after 70 CE) and considers it "inferior" to Syr Baruch.

1872   Prätorius, F.   "Das apokryphische Buch Baruch im Aethiopischen," ZEITSCHRIFT FÜR WISSENSCHAFTLICHE THEOLOGIE 15, 230ff. German translation of Dillman's eth. (A. Hilgenfeld provides an introductory footnote with primarily bibliographic comments, and nothing on date, origin, etc.) In the 1874 vol of ZWT, H. Sachesse appends some critical remarks on details of the German translation (268f).

1877   König, E.   "Der Reste der Worte Baruchs," THEOLOGISCHE STUDIEN UND KRITIKEN 50, 318ff. Another, independent German translation of Dillman's eth. König considers eth to be closer to the original than is the Greek MS published by Ceriani in 1868.

1879   Kneucker, J. J.   DAS BUCH BARUCH (Leipzig), 196f. Follows Dillmann on origin and date of ParJer, and calls it a tasteless imitation of Syriac Baruch, also dependent on Asc Isa.

1883   Dillmann's article in the Herzog REALENCYC. (see above, under 1866).

1885   Guidi. On the Abimelech story in ParJer (so Huber, below 1910 "Guidi, p. 444").

1887 Schürer, E. (Early view; see below 1890, 1909).
1889 Harris, J. R. THE REST OF THE WORDS OF BARUCH = Haverford College Studies 2 (London), 1-46 on introductory matters, followed by a critical edition of the Greek text. ParJer was written by a Jewish-Christian of Jerusalem in 136 CE as "the church's eirenicon to the synagogue." It is dependent on Syriac Baruch, 4 Ezra, Asc Isa, and probably also Gospel of John.
1890 Schürer, E. Review of Harris' edition in THEOLOGISCHE LITERATURZEITUNG 15, 81-83. Harris' hypothesis on origin of ParJer is unconvincing. It is a Jewish work with a clumsy Christian ending. The demand for separation from Gentiles (and especially for dissolution of mixed marriages) is a peculiarly Jewish concern. Evidence for dating ParJer is insufficient. [Cf the earlier view of Schürer in his GESCHICHTE^2 (= English 2.3[1891], 92) that ParJer is a Christian work borrowing from Syr Baruch!]
1891 Bonwetsch, N. Review of Harris' edition in THEOLOGISCHES LITERATURBLATT 12, 422-424. The bulk of the review is devoted to comments on and a collation of the slav ParJer materials.
1891 Gaster, M. CHRESTOMATHIE ROMANA 1 (Leipzig), 147-149 (Jeremiah-Baruch-Abimelech legends in Rumanian; also pp. 253-256), 311 (fragment of Dorotheus' SYNOPSIS in Rumanian).
1892 Kozak, E. "Bibliographische Uebersicht der biblisch-apokryphen bei den Slaven," JAHRBÜCHER FÜR PROTESTANTISCHE THEOLOGIE 18, 138.
1893 Bonwetsch, N. Appendix on Slavic materials in A. Harnack, GESCHICHTE DER ALTCHRISTLICHEN LITERATUR BIS EUSEBIUS (Leipzig) 1.2, 916.
1893 Harnack, A. GESCHICHTE 1.2 (see preceding entry), 852. ParJer is treated as a late (possibly 4th century CE) Christian work.
1893 Vassiliev, A. ANECDOTA GRAECO-BYZANTINA 1 (Moscow), 308-316. Edition of Greek MS v of the SHORT FORM of ParJer.
1893 Basset, R. LES APOCRYPHES ÉTHIOPIENS TRADUITS EN FRANCAIS 1: LE LIVRE DE BARUCH ET LA LÉGENDE DE JÉRÉMIE (Paris).
1893 Kohler, K. "The Pre-Talmudic Haggada. B. The Second Baruch or rather the Jeremiah Apocalypse," JEWISH QUARTERLY REVIEW 5, 407-419. ParJer is a Jewish haggadic work with many rabbinic parallels, solely dictated by the messianic hope of the Jews and manifesting a national spirit in its anti-Samaritan thrust. It was written not long after the destruction of the second temple and is much *older* than Syriac Baruch. Kohler claims to find traces of the original Jewish thought behind the clumsy Christian interpolations, even in the corrupt and defective apocalyptic part of the book.
1895 Karapet. Edition of Armenian in ZEITSCHRIFT DES ARMENISCHEN PATRIARCHATS.
1896 Josepheantz, H. S. Edition of Armenian non-canonical Jewish texts (Venice), 349-363. An English translation of this material by H. Issaverdentz, THE UNCANONICAL WRITINGS OF THE OLD TESTAMENT, appeared in 1901 (1907^2).
1896 Charles, R. H. THE APOCALYPSE OF BARUCH TRANSLATED FROM THE SYRIAC (London), xviii-xix. ParJer was written in Greek in the 2nd century, and seems to be a Jewish work recast, in parts. It is deeply indebted to Syr Baruch.
1897 James, M. R. APOCRYPHA ANECDOTA 2 = Texts and Studies 5.1 (Cambridge), liii (cf also lxxi). Repeats Harris' ideas about ParJer, and suggests that the Greek apocalypse of Baruch (usually = 3 Baruch) knew ParJer.
1900 Ryssel, V. Discussion in Kautzsch, DIE APOKRYPHEN UND PSEUDEPIGRAPHEN DES ALTEN TESTAMENTS (Tübingen) 2, 402f and 447. Follows Schürer on the origin of ParJer, and Charles on parallels with Syr Baruch. Also discusses the relation between ParJer and the Greek apocalypse of Baruch.

1901 Gröber, G. GRUNDRISS DER ROMANISCHEN PHILOLOGIE 2.3 (Strassburg), 399f. Comments briefly on the Rumanian version of ParJer.
1903 Kohler, K. "Ebed-Melech," JEWISH ENCYCLOPEDIA 5, 29-30. Recounts the story of Abimelech according to ParJer.
1904 Ginzberg, L. "Jeremiah," JEWISH ENCYCLOPEDIA 7, 100-102. Mentions ParJer among various Jeremiah traditions.
1905 Beer, G. "Pseudepigraphen des AT" (No. 35 = Paralipomena Jeremiae), REALENCYKLOPÄDIE FÜR PROTESTANTISCHE THEOLOGIE UND KIRCHE[3] 16, 262. Follows Schürer on origin of ParJer (basically Jewish, with Christian interpolation), and suggests date at end of 1st century or in opening decades of the 2nd (after Syr Baruch, which it uses). [The English translation of this material in the NEW SCHAFF-HERZOG ENCYCLOPEDIA is inaccurate.]
1909 Schürer, E. GESCHICHTE DES JÜDISCHEN VOLKES IM ZEITALTER JESU CHRISTI[4] (Leipzig), 393-395. Adds nothing to his 1890 comments (already in 1898[3] ed.).
1910 Huber, M. DIE WANDERLEGENDE VON DEN SIEBENSCHLÄFERN (Leipzig), 408f. Reports dating hypotheses of Dillmann (3rd century or later) and Harris. Notes that Gaster argues for Christian origin, but Huber affirms idea of Jewish core with Christian interpolations. Cites Guidi on 3-4th century date of ParJer (later than Syr Baruch and Asc Isa), with Abimelech legend much older.
1913 Charles, R. H. THE APOCRYPHA AND PSEUDEPIGRAPHA OF THE OLD TESTAMENT IN ENGLISH (Oxford) 2, 471 and 528. The first reference adds nothing to Charles' 1896 views. The second, by H. M. Hughes, adds nothing to Ryssel's 1900 treatment.
1913 Ginzberg, L. THE LEGENDS OF THE JEWS 4 (Philadelphia), 318-320. Summarizes contents of ParJer in relation to different personalities and traditions.
1920 Stählin, O. "Die hellenistisch-jüdische Literatur," in W. von Christ, GESCHICHTE DER GRIECHISCHEN LITERATUR[6] 2.1 (Munich), 586-587. Follows Schürer position.
1924 Violet, B. DIE APOKALYPSEN DES EZRA UND DES BARUCH = Die griechischen christlichen Schriftsteller der ersten drei Jahrhunderte 32 (Leipzig), xciv. Mentions ParJer along with other Baruch literature.
1926 Bousset, W. and Gressman, H. DIE RELIGION DES JUDENTUMS IN SPÄTHELLENISTISCHEN ZEITALTER[3] (Tübingen), 37. Follows Schürer position.
1927 Harris, J. R. Remarks in WOODBROOKE STUDIES 1, 133 and 135f. Rejects the notion that ParJer is a "bona-fide Jewish document" (refers to views of S. Davidson).
1928 Riessler, P. ALTJÜDISCHES SCHRIFTTUM AUSSERHALB DER BIBEL (Augsburg), 1323. Follows Schürer position.
1928 Frey, J.-B. "Apocryphes de l'Ancien Testament" (No. 16. Les Paralipomènes de Jérémie), in DICTIONNAIRE DE LA BIBLE. Supplement 1, 454f. ParJer was written by a Jew (using Syr Baruch) around the mid-2nd century. Greek was the original language (following Charles).
1945 Kilpatrick, G. D. "Acts vii.52: *ELEUSIS*," JOURNAL OF THEOLOGICAL STUDIES 46, 141. ParJer was written in Hebrew around the time 70-130 CE (probably closer to 130), and taken over by Christians by 130. Discusses Greek variants in ParJer 3.11 *syneleusis/synteleia*.
1949 Pfeiffer, R. H. HISTORY OF NEW TESTAMENT TIMES . . . (New York), 61 and 74. ParJer is listed under "works in Aramaic, A.D. 1-100: legends."
1950 Lods, A. HISTOIRE DE LA LITTERATURE HÉBRAIQUE ET JUIVE (Paris), 998. ParJer mentioned in straightforward list.

1957 Klausner, J. (Hebrew) MEḤKARIM ḤADASHIM U-MEKOROT ATTIKIM, 90-117.
1961 Meyer, R. "Paralipomena Jeremiae," in DIE RELIGION IN GESCHICHTE UND GEGENWART³ 5, 102f. Mentions the anti-Samaritan motif and suggests a date of ca 100-140 CE for Christian editing of Jewish original.
1963 Licht, J. Hebrew article with English summary on ParJer, in the ANNUAL OF BAR-ILAN UNIVERSITY: STUDIES IN JUDAICA AND THE HUMANITIES 1 = Pinkhos Ghurgin Memorial Volume (Jerusalem), 66-72 and xxi-xxii. ParJer represents a little-known genre of Hebrew literature—the popular, theologically unambitious, fully narrative legend. It was written by a Palestinian Jew around 136 CE and is linked to the Bar Kochba revolt. The Greek is a fairly free paraphrase of a Hebrew original.
1967 Delling, G. JUDISCHE LEHRE UND FRÖMMIGKEIT IN DEN PARALIPOMENA JEREMIAE = Beihefte zur Zeitschrift für die alttestamentliche Wissenschaft 100 (Berlin). Examines various themes and/or phrases in ParJer and concludes that behind the present text lies a basically Jewish book of exhortation, instruction, and edification, from the hand of a single author (up to ParJer 9.11 = Harris 9.9). It was written originally in the "Palestinian vernacular" and represents a type of Judaism similar to the later Pharisaic position. The work was translated into a "semitized" Greek, probably by a Palestinian, and a Christian ending was added later. ParJer dates from approximately the first third of the 2nd century. [For some significant comments and reactions, see the reviews by O. S. Wintermute, CATHOLIC BIBLICAL QUARTERLY 30 (1968), 442-445 (on relatiton to "gnosis," possible Christian "glosses" in 1.1-9.11, evidence of complicated redactional history, etc.), and M.-P. Bogaert, REVUE BENEDICTINE 78 (1968), 345f (possibility of a Jewish-Christian origin, question of what was the original ending).]
1968 Stuhlmacher, P. DAS PAULINISCHE EVANGELIUM. 1: VORGESCHICHTE (Göttingen), 177 ff n. 2. Follows Delling on date, origin and composition of ParJer as introduction to long note on "Jewish usage" of *euaggelizesthai* (= *BASAR*) and associated terms in ParJer.
1969 Bogaert, P. APOCALYPSE DE BARUCH = Sources Chrétiennes 144-145 (Paris), *passim* but especially 1, 177-221 (ch. 5) on "Les Paralipomèna Jeremiae et l'Apocalypse syriaque de Baruch." ParJer depends on Syr Baruch. The theological content of ParJer imparts a certain unity to the various blocks of material. Accepts Harris' date of 136 CE for ParJer, and suggests that it was written to Jewish-Christians by a Jewish-Christian, while admitting the possibility that it is a Jewish work edited by a Christian sometime after 135.
1970 Denis, A.-M. "Les Paralipomènes de Jérémie = ch. 7 of INTRODUCTION AUX PSEUDEPIGRAPHIES GRECS D'ANCIEN TESTAMENT = Studia in Veteris Testamenti Pseudepigrapha (Leiden), 70-78. After noting important MSS, editions, translations, and discussions, Denis concludes that ParJer is a basically Jewish document with Christian reworking, written between 70-130 CE possibly in Greek, or more likely Hebrew, and using Syr Baruch.
1971 Stone, M. E. "Baruch, Rest of the Words of," in ENCYCLOPAEDIA JUDAICA 4, 276f. ParJer is Jewish material reworked by Christians. It depends on Syr Baruch and dates after 70 CE, perhaps in the reign of Hadrian (note its anti-Samaritan polemic).

Note: We have intentionally omitted reference to some treatments (e.g. in Encylopedia articles on Jeremiah or Baruch or Pseudepigrapha) in which ParJer is simply listed without significant comment. We hope that significant omissions will be brought to our attention speedily.

PARALEIPOMENA JEREMIOU

ΤΑ ΠΑΡΑΛΕΙΠΟΜΕΝΑ ΙΕΡΕΜΙΟΥ ΤΟΥ ΠΡΟΦΗΤΟΥ

1.1 Ἐγένετο, ἡνίκα ἠχμαλωτεύθησαν οἱ υἱοὶ Ἰσραὴλ ἀπὸ τοῦ βασιλέως τῶν Χαλδαίων, ἐλάλησεν ὁ θεὸς πρὸς Ἰερεμίαν λέγων·

Ἰερεμία, ὁ ἐκλεκτός μου, ἀνάστα, καὶ ἔξελθε ἐκ τῆς πόλεως ταύτης, σὺ καὶ

Βαρούχ· ἐπειδὴ ἀπολῶ αὐτὴν διὰ τὸ πλῆθος τῶν

.2 ἁμαρτιῶν τῶν κατοικούντων ἐν αὐτῇ. Αἱ γὰρ προσευχαὶ ὑμῶν ὡς στῦλος

ἑδραῖός ἐστιν ἐν μέσῳ αὐτῆς, καὶ ὡς τεῖχος ἀδαμάντινον περικυκλοῦν αὐτήν.

.3 Νῦν οὖν ἀναστάντες ἐξέλθατε πρὸ τοῦ ἡ δύναμις τῶν Χαλδαίων κυκλώσει αὐτήν.

.4 Καὶ ἀπεκρίθη Ἰερεμίας, λέγων·

Παρακαλῶ σε, κύριε, ἐπίτρεψόν μοι τῷ δούλῳ σου λαλῆσαι ἐνώτιόν σου.

.5 Εἶπεν δὲ αὐτῷ ὁ κύριος·

Λάλει, ὁ ἐκλεκτός μου Ἰερεμίας.

.6 Καὶ ἐλάλησεν Ἰερεμίας, λέγων·

Κύριε παντοκράτωρ, παραδίδως τὴν πόλιν τὴν ἐκλεκτὴν εἰς χεῖρας τῶν

Χαλδαίων, ἵνα καυχήσηται ὁ βασιλεὺς μετὰ τοῦ πλήθους τοῦ λαοῦ αὐτοῦ,

καὶ εἴπῃ ὅτι, "Ἴσχυσα ἐπὶ τὴν ἱερὰν πόλιν τοῦ θεοῦ;

.7 Μή, κύριέ μου· ἀλλ' εἰ θέλημά σού ἐστιν, ἐκ τῶν χειρῶν σου ἀφανισθήτω.

.8 Καὶ εἶπε κύριος τῷ Ἰερεμίᾳ·

Ἐπειδὴ σὺ ἐκλεκτός μου εἶ, ἀνάστα καὶ ἔξελθε ἐκ τῆς πόλεως ταύτης, σὺ καὶ

Βαρούχ· ἐπειδὴ ἀπολῶ αὐτὴν διὰ τὸ πλῆθος τῶν

.9 ἁμαρτιῶν τῶν κατοικούντων ἐν αὐτῇ. Οὔτε γὰρ ὁ βασιλεύς, οὔτε ἡ δύναμις αὐτοῦ,

δυνήσεται εἰσελθεῖν εἰς αὐτήν, εἰ μὴ ἐγὼ πρῶτος ἀνοίξω τὰς πύλας αὐτῆς.

.10 Ἀνάστηθι οὖν, καὶ ἀπελθὲ πρὸς Βαρούχ, καὶ ἀπάγγειλον αὐτῷ τὰ ῥήματα ταῦτα.

.11 Καὶ ἀναστάντες ἕκτην ὥραν τῆς νυκτός, ἔλθετε ἐπὶ τὰ τείχη τῆς πόλεως,

καὶ δείξω ὑμῖν ὅτι ἐὰν μή τι ἐγὼ πρῶτος ἀφανίσω τὴν πόλιν, οὐ δύνανται εἰσελθεῖν εἰς αὐτήν.

.12 Ταῦτα εἰπὼν ὁ κύριος, ἀπῆλθεν ἀπὸ τοῦ Ἰερεμίου.

THE THINGS OMITTED FROM JEREMIAH THE PROPHET

1.1 It came to pass, when the children of Israel were taken captive by the king of the Chaldeans, that God spoke to Jeremiah saying:
Jeremiah, my chosen one, arise and depart from this city, you and Baruch, since I am going to destroy it because of the multitude of
.2 the sins of those who dwell in it. For your prayers are like a solid pillar in its midst, and like an indestructible wall surrounding it.
.3 Now, then, arise and depart before the host of the Chaldeans surrounds it.
.4 And Jeremiah answered, saying:
I beseech you, Lord, permit me, your servant, to speak in your presence.
.5 And the Lord said to him:
Speak, my chosen one Jeremiah.
.6 And Jeremiah spoke, saying:
Lord Almighty, would you deliver the chosen city into the hands of the Chaldeans, so that the king with the multitude of his people might boast and say: "I have prevailed over the holy city of God"?
.7 No, my Lord, but if it is your will, let it be destroyed by your hands.
.8 And the Lord said to Jeremiah:
Since you are my chosen one, arise and depart from this city, you and Baruch, for I am going to destroy it because of the multitude of the
.9 sins of those who dwell in it. For neither the king nor his host will
.10 be able to enter it unless I first open its gates. Arise, then, and go
.11 to Baruch, and tell him these words. And when you have arisen at the sixth hour of the night, go out on the city walls and I will show you that unless I first destroy the city, they cannot enter it.
.12 When the Lord had said this, he departed from Jeremiah.

title so BA(H)F(cf arm) C : Narrative concerning the Captivity of Jerusalem W(J) (cf POSIM) : The Rest of the Words of Baruch . . . eth
1.1 It came to pass—captive ABarm Ceth (with some minor variations) :
It came to pass in those days when the sons of Israel were provoking the Lord God to anger and were about to be taken captive and their city devastated. P (= Oxford Bodl. B. 240.2)
.1 my chosen one ABarm P eth: om C hist
.4 your servant ABarm P eth: om C hist
.6 multitude of his people AB eth: his multitude P: multitude of his troops arm (cf hist): om C
.11 destroy the city arm P eth (cf C): + and I will open (it) AB (cf hist)
.12 he departed from Jeremiah AB P eth: + into heaven C [see 3.17]: to Jeremiah he departed from him arm hist

2.1   Δράμων δὲ Ἱερεμίας ἀνήγγειλε ταῦτα τῷ βαροὺχ, καὶ
            ἐλθόντες
      εἰς τὸν ναὸν τοῦ θεοῦ διέρρηξεν ὁ Ἱερεμίας τὰ ἱμάτια αὐτοῦ
          καὶ ἐπέθηκεν χοῦν ἐπὶ
      τὴν κεφαλὴν αὐτοῦ καὶ εἰσῆλθεν εἰς τὸ ἁγιαστήριον τοῦ θεοῦ.
          Ἰδὼν δὲ αὐτὸν ὁ Βαροὺχ
      χοῦν πεπασμένον ἐπὶ τὴν   κεφαλὴν αὐτοῦ, καὶ τὰ ἱμάτια αὐτοῦ
          διερρωγότα, ἔκραξε
      φωνῇ μεγάλῃ, λέγων·

            Πάτερ Ἱερεμία, τί ἐστι σοι, ἢ ποῖον ἁμάρτημα ἐποίησεν ὁ
                λαός;
 .3   (Ἐπειδὴ ὅταν ἡμάρτανεν ὁ λαός, χοῦν ἔπασσεν ἐπὶ τὴν κεφαλὴν
            αὐτοῦ ὁ Ἱερεμίας,
      καὶ ηὔχετο ὑπὲρ τοῦ λαοῦ, ἕως ἂν ἀφεθῇ αὐτῷ ἡ ἁμαρτία.)
 .4   Ἠρώτησε δὲ αὐτὸν ὁ Βαροὺχ, λέγων·
            Πάτερ, τί ἐστι τοῦτο;
 .5   Εἶπε δὲ αὐτῷ Ἱερεμίας·
            Ψύλαξαι τοῦ σχίσαι τὰ ἱμάτιά σου,
                ἀλλὰ μᾶλλον σχίσωμεν τὰς καρδίας ἡμῶν·
            Καὶ μὴ ἀντλήσωμεν ὕδωρ ἐπὶ τὰς ποτίστρας,
                ἀλλὰ κλαύσωμεν καὶ γεμίσωμεν αὐτὰς δακρύων·
            ὅτι οὐ μὴ ἐλεήσῃ κύριος τὸν λαὸν τοῦτον
 .6   Καὶ εἶπε Βαρούχ·
            Πάτερ Ἱερεμία, τί γέγονε;
 .7   Καὶ εἶπεν Ἱερεμίας ὅτι,
            Ὁ θεὸς παραδίδωσι τὴν πόλιν εἰς χεῖρας τοῦ βασιλέως τῶν
                Χαλδαίων,
            τοῦ αἰχμαλωτεῦσαι τὸν λαὸν εἰς Βαβυλῶνα.
 .8   Ἀκούσας δὲ ταῦτα Βαροὺχ, διέρρηξε καὶ αὐτὸς τὰ ἱμάτια αὐτοῦ,
            καὶ εἶπε·
            Πάτερ Ἱερεμία, τίς σοι ἐδήλωσε τοῦτο;
 .9   Καὶ εἶπεν αὐτῷ Ἱερεμίας·
            Ἔκδεξαι μικρὸν μετ' ἐμοῦ ἕως ὥρας ἕκτης τῆς νυκτός,
            ἵνα γνῷς ὅτι ἀληθές ἐστι τὸ ῥῆμα τοῦτο.
 .10   Ἔμειναν οὖν ἀμφότεροι ἐν τῷ θυσιαστηρίῳ κλαίοντες, καὶ ἦσαν
      διερρωγότα τὰ ἱμάτια αὐτῶν.

… 2.1-10

2.1 And Jeremiah ran and told these things to Baruch; and as they went into the temple of God, Jeremiah tore his garments and put dust on his
.2 head and entered the holy place of God. And when Baruch saw him with dust sprinkled on his head and his garments torn, he cried out in a loud voice, saying:

Father Jeremiah, what are you doing? What sin has the people committed?

.3 (For whenever the people sinned, Jeremiah would sprinkle dust on his head
.4 and would pray for the people until their sin was forgiven.) So Baruch asked him, saying:

Father, what is this?

.5 And Jeremiah said to him:

Refrain from rending your garments—
rather, let us rend our hearts!
And let us not draw water for the troughs,
but let us weep and fill them with tears!
For the Lord will not have mercy on this people.

.6 And Baruch said:

Father Jeremiah, what has happened?

.7 And Jeremiah said:

God is delivering the city into the hands of the king of the Chaldeans, to take the people captive into Babylon.

.8 And when Baruch heard these things, he also tore his garments and said:

Father Jeremiah, who has made this known to you?

.9 And Jeremiah said to him:

Stay with me awhile, until the sixth hour of the night, so that you may know that this word is true.

.10 Therefore they both remained in the altar-area weeping, and their garments were torn.

2.1 Jeremiah—temple of God ABarm P hist: om Ceth (possibly correctly; see what follows!)
.1 and entered the holy place of God C (cf eth): and both began to weep over (in, B) the holy place of God B P: A omits context
.4 Father P Ceth: om ABarm
.7 the king of ABarm eth: om P C
.10 and their garments were torn arm: + and earth was on their heads AB P: om Ceth

3.1 Ὡς δὲ ἐγένετο ἡ ὥρα τῆς νυκτὸς, καθὼς εἶπεν ὁ κύριος τῷ Ἰερεμίᾳ,
ἦλθον ὁμοῦ ἐπὶ τὰ τείχη τῆς πόλεως Ἰερεμίας καὶ Βαροὺχ.
.2 Καὶ ἰδοὺ ἐγένετο φωνὴ σαλπίγγων, καὶ ἐξῆλθον ἄγγελοι ἐκ τοῦ οὐρανοῦ, κατέχοντες λαμπάδας ἐν ταῖς χερσὶν αὐτῶν, καὶ ἔστησαν ἐπὶ τὰ τείχη
.3 τῆς πόλεως. Ἰδόντες δὲ αὐτοὺς Ἰερεμίας καὶ Βαροὺχ, ἔκλαυσαν, λέγοντες·
Νῦν ἐγνώκαμεν ὅτι ἀληθές ἐστι τὸ ῥῆμα.
.4 Παρεκάλεσε δὲ Ἰερεμίας τοὺς ἀγγέλους, λέγων·
Παρακαλῶ ὑμᾶς μὴ ἀπολέσθαι τὴν πόλιν ἄρτι, ἕως ἂν λαλήσω πρὸς κύριον ῥῆμα.
.5 Ἐλάλησεν δὲ κύριος τοῖς ἀγγέλοις, λέγων·
Μὴ ἀπολέσητε τὴν πόλιν ἕως ἂν λαλήσω πρὸς τὸν ἐκλεκτόν μου Ἰερεμίαν.
.6 Τότε Ἰερεμίας ἐλάλησεν, λέγων·
Δέομαι, κύριε, κέλευσόν με λαλῆσαι ἐνώπιόν σου.
.7 Καὶ εἶπε κύριος·
Λάλει, ὁ ἐκλεκτός μου Ἰερεμίας.
.8 Καὶ εἶπεν Ἰερεμίας·
Ἰδοὺ νῦν, κύριε, ἐγνώκαμεν ὅτι παραδίδως τὴν πόλιν εἰς χεῖρας τῶν ἐχθρῶν αὐτῆς, καὶ ἀπαροῦσι τὸν λαὸν εἰς Βαβυλῶνα.
.9 Τί θέλεις ποιήσω τὰ ἅγια σκεύη τῆς λειτουργίας,
.10 Καὶ εἶπεν αὐτῷ ὁ κύριος·
Ἆρον αὐτὰ, καὶ παράδος αὐτὰ τῇ γῇ λέγων·
Ἄκουε, γῆ, τῆς φωνῆς τοῦ κτίσαντός σε,
ὁ πλάσας σε ἐν τῇ περιουσίᾳ τῶν ὑδάτων,
ὁ σφραγίσας σε ἐν ἑπτὰ σφραγῖσιν ἐν ἑπτὰ καιροῖς,
καὶ μετὰ ταῦτα λήψῃ τὴν ὡραιότητά σου·
.11 Φύλαξον τὰ σκεύη τῆς λειτουργίας ἕως τῆς συνελεύσεως τοῦ ἠγαπημένου.

THE THINGS OMITTED FROM JEREMIAH

3.1-11

3.1 And when the hour of the night arrived, as the Lord had told Jeremiah, they came up together on the walls of the city, Jeremiah and Baruch.
.2 And behold, there came a sound of trumpets; and angels emerged from heaven holding torches in their hands, and they set them on the walls of
.3 the city. And when Jeremiah and Baruch saw them, they wept, saying:
Now we know that the word is true!
.4 And Jeremiah besought the angels, saying:
I beseech you, do not destroy the city yet, until I say something to the Lord.
.5 And the Lord spoke to the angels, saying:
Do not destroy the city until I speak to my chosen one, Jeremiah.
.6 Then Jeremiah spoke, saying:
I beg you, Lord, bid me to speak in your presence.
.7 And the Lord said:
Speak, my chosen one Jeremiah.
.8 And Jeremiah said:
Behold, Lord, now we know that you are delivering the city into the hands of its enemies, and they will take the people away to Babylon.
.9 What do you want me to do with the holy vessels of the temple service?
.10 And the Lord said to him:
Take them and consign them to the earth, saying:
Hear, Earth, the voice of your creator
who formed you in the abundance of waters,
who sealed you with seven seals for seven epochs,
and after this you will receive your ornaments (?)—
.11 Guard the vessels of the temple service until the gathering of the beloved.

3.1 the hour of the night AB: the hour C: the day P: the 6th watch arm: the 6th (var 12th) hour of the night eth hist
.1 Jeremiah and Baruch ABarm P: om Ceth hist
.4 the Lord arm C hist: my Lord P: Lord God eth: God most high AB
.5 this entire verse is lacking in AB (cf hist), but included by arm P Ceth
.6 Jeremiah spoke saying arm P eth hist: he said crying AB: om context C
.10 to the earth ABarm P hist: + and to the altar area Ceth [see 3.18 var]
.10 who formed you Ceth: om ABarm P
.10 with seven seals AB P eth: om arm C
.10 and after this you will receive (will take away, arm) AB (arm) P: + the way C: Take eth
.11 until the gathering (C at 4.4) eth men-gk: until the coming arm men-arm: until the completion/consummation AB P: the C text appears at 4.4f, where some material also is repeated that is found in the conflated C text of 3.11 (apparently C has transposed material to 3.11 from 4.4f)

.12 Ἐλάλησε δὲ Ἰεμεμίας λέγων·
Παρακαλῶ σε, κύριε, δεῖξόν μοι τί ποιήσω Ἀβιμέλεχ τῷ
Αἰθίοπι, ὅτι πολλὰς εὐεργεσίας ἐποίησε τῷ δούλῳ σου
Ἰερεμίᾳ.
.13 Ὅτι αὐτὸς ἀνέσπασέ με ἐκ τοῦ λάκκου τοῦ βορβόρου· καὶ
οὐ θέλω αὐτὸν ἵνα
ἴδῃ τὸν ἀφανισμὸν τῆς πόλεως ταύτης καὶ τὴν ἐρήμωσιν,
ἀλλ' ἵνα
ἐλεήσῃς αὐτὸν καὶ μὴ λυπηθῇ.
.14 Καὶ εἶπε κύριος τῷ Ἰερεμίᾳ·
Ἀπόστειλον αὐτὸν εἰς τὸν ἀμπελῶνα τοῦ Ἀγρίππα, καὶ ἐν
τῇ σκιᾷ τοῦ ὄρους ἐγὼ
σκεπάσω αὐτόν, ἕως οὗ ἐπιστρέψω τὸν λαὸν εἰς τὴν πόλιν.
.15 Σὺ δὲ Ἰερεμίας, ἄπελθε μετὰ τοῦ λαοῦ σου εἰς Βαβυλῶνα,
καὶ μεῖνον μετ'
αὐτῶν εὐαγγελιζόμενος αὐτοῖς ἕως οὗ ἐπιστρέψω αὐτοὺς εἰς
τὴν πόλιν.
.16 Κατάλειψον δὲ τὸν Βαροὺχ ὧδε, ἕως οὗ λαλήσω αὐτῷ.
.17 Ταῦτα εἰπὼν ὁ κύριος, ἀνέβη ἀπὸ Ἰερεμίου εἰς τὸν οὐρανόν.
.18 Ἰερεμίας δὲ καὶ Βαροὺχ εἰσῆλθον εἰς τὸ ἁγιαστήριον,
καὶ ἐπάραντες τὰ
σκεύη τῆς λειτουργίας παρέδωκαν αὐτὰ τῇ γῇ, καθὼς
.19 ἐλάλησεν αὐτοῖς ὁ κύριος. Καὶ εὐθέως κατέπιεν αὐτὰ ἡ γῆ.
.20 Ἐκάθισαν δὲ οἱ δύο, καὶ ἔκλαυσαν.
.21 Πρωΐας δὲ γενομένης, ἀπέστειλεν Ἰερεμίας τὸν Ἀβιμέλεχ,
λέγων·
Ἆρον τὸν κόφινον, καὶ ἄπελθε εἰς τὸ χωρίον τοῦ Ἀγρίππα
διὰ τῆς ὁδοῦ τοῦ ὄρους,
καὶ ἐνεγκὼν ὀλίγα σῦκα, δίδου τοῖς νοσοῦσι τοῦ λαοῦ· ὅτι
ἐπὶ σὲ ἡ εὐφρασία τοῦ κυρίου, καὶ ἐπὶ τὴν κεφαλήν σου
ἡ δόξα.
.22 Καὶ ταῦτα εἰπὼν Ἰερεμίας ἀπέλυσεν αὐτόν· Ἀβιμέλεχ δὲ
ἐπορεύθη καθὰ εἶπεν αὐτῷ.

THE THINGS OMITTED FROM JEREMIAH 19

3.12-22

3.12 And Jeremiah spoke, saying:
I beseech you, Lord, show me what I should do for Abimelech the Ethiopian, for he has done many kindnesses to your servant Jeremiah.
.13 For he pulled me out of the miry pit; and I do not wish that he should see the destruction and desolation of this city, but that you should be merciful to him and that he should not be grieved.
.14 And the Lord said to Jeremiah:
Send him to the vineyard of Agrippa, and I will hide him in the shadow of the mountain until I cause the people to return to the city.
.15 And you, Jeremiah, go with your people into Babylon and stay with them, preaching to them, until I cause them to return to the city.
.16 But leave Baruch here until I speak with him.
.17 When he had said these things, the Lord ascended from Jeremiah into heaven.
.18 But Jeremiah and Baruch entered the holy place, and taking the vessels of the temple service, they consigned them to the earth as
.19 the Lord had told them. And immediately the earth swallowed them.
.20 And they both sat down and wept.
.21 And when morning came, Jeremiah sent Abimelech, saying:
Take a basket and go to the estate of Agrippa by the mountain road, and bring back some figs to give to the sick among the people; for the favor of the Lord is on you and his glory is on your head.
.22 And when he had said this, Jeremiah sent him away; and Abimelech went as he told him.

3.12 spoke ABarm eth: + to the Lord P C hist
.12 to your servant Jeremiah P: to your servant arm hist: to Jeremiah AB: to the people and to your servant (+ Jeremiah eth) C (eth)
.12 miry arm Ceth hist: om AB P
.15 And you arm P eth hist: And the Lord said AB: om context C
.18 to the earth ABarm P eth hist: + and to the altar area C [see 3.10 var]
.20 they both Ceth: together they ABarm P
.22 And when—away ABarm P (cf hist): om Ceth

4.1-12
4.1 Πρωΐας δὲ γενομένης, ἰδοὺ ἡ δύναμις τῶν Χαλδαίων ἐκύκλωσε
.2 τὴν πόλιν. Ἐσάλπισεν δὲ ὁ μέγας ἄγγελος, λέγων·
Εἰσέλθατε εἰς τὴν πόλιν ἡ δύναμις τῶν Χαλδαίων· ἰδοὺ γὰρ
.3 ἠνεῴχθη ὑμῖν ἡ πύλη. Εἰσελθέτω οὖν ὁ βασιλεὺς μετὰ
τοῦ πλήθους αὐτοῦ, καὶ αἰχμαλωτευσάτω πάντα τὸν λαόν.
.4 Ἰερεμίας δὲ ἄρας τὰς κλεῖδας τοῦ ναοῦ, ἐξῆλθεν ἔξω τῆς
πόλεως,
καὶ ἔρριψεν αὐτὰς ἐνώπιον τοῦ ἡλίου, λέγων·
Σοὶ λέγω, ἥλιε, λάβε τὰς κλεῖδας τοῦ ναοῦ τοῦ θεοῦ,
καὶ φύλαξον
αὐτὰς ἕως ἡμέρας, ἐν ᾗ ἐξετάσει σε κύριος περὶ αὐτῶν.
.5 Διότι ἡμεῖς οὐχ εὑρέθημεν ἄξιοι τοῦ φυλάξαι αὐτάς,
ὅτι ἐπίτροποι τοῦ ψεύδους ἐγενήθημεν.
.6 Ἔτι κλαίοντος Ἰερεμίου τὸν λαόν, ἐξένεγκαν αὐτόν
μετὰ τοῦ λαοῦ εἵλκοντες εἰς Βαβυλῶνα.
.7 Ὁ δὲ Βαροὺχ ἐπέθηκε χοῦν ἐπὶ τὴν κεφαλὴν αὐτοῦ,
καὶ ἐκάθισε, καὶ ἔκλαυσε
τὸν θρῆνον τοῦτον, λέγων·
Διὰ τί ἠρημώθη Ἰερουσαλήμ; Διὰ τὰς ἁμαρτίας του ἠγαπημένου
λαοῦ παρεδόθη εἰς χεῖρας ἐχθρῶν, διὰ
.8 τὰς ἁμαρτίας ἡμῶν καὶ τοῦ λαοῦ. Ἀλλὰ μὴ καυχάσθωσαν οἱ
παράνομοι, καὶ
εἴπωσιν ὅτι,
Ἰσχύσαμεν λαβεῖν τὴν πόλιν τοῦ θεοῦ ἐν τῇ δυνάμει
ἡμῶν·
.9 ἀλλὰ διὰ τὰς ἁμαρτίας ἡμῶν παρεδόθη ὑμῖν. Ὁ δὲ θεὸς
ἡμῶν οἰκτειρήσει
ἡμᾶς, καὶ ἐπιστρέψει ἡμᾶς εἰς τὴν πόλιν ἡμῶν· ὑμεῖς δὲ
ζωὴν οὐχ ἕξετε.
.10 Μακάριοί εἰσιν οἱ πατέρες ἡμῶν, Ἀβραὰμ, Ἰσαὰκ καὶ
Ἰακώβ, ὅτι ἐξῆλθον
ἐκ τοῦ κόσμου τούτου, καὶ οὐκ εἶδον τὸν ἀφανισμὸν τῆς
πόλεως ταύτης.
.11 Ταῦτα εἰπὼν Βαροὺχ ἐξῆλθεν ἔξω τῆς πόλεως κλαίων καὶ λέγων
ὅτι
Λυπούμενος διὰ σὲ, Ἰερουσαλὴμ, ἐξῆλθον ἀπὸ σοῦ.
.12 Καὶ ἔμεινεν ἐν μνημείῳ καθεζόμενος, τῶν ἀγγέλων ἐρχομένων
πρὸς αὐτὸν, καὶ
ἐκδιηγουμένων αὐτῷ περὶ πάντων ὧν ὁ κύριος ἐμήνυεν αὐτῷ
δι' αὐτῶν.

4.1 And when morning came, behold the host of the Chaldeans surrounded
.2 the city. And the great angel trumpeted, saying:
Enter the city, host of the Chaldeans; for behold, the gate is
.3 opened for you. Therefore let the king enter, with his multitudes, and let him take all the people captive.
4. But taking the keys of the temple, Jeremiah went outside the city and threw them away in the presence of the sun, saying:
I say to you, Sun, take the keys of the temple of God and guard them until the day in which the Lord asks you for them.
.5 For we have not been found worthy to keep them, for we have become unfaithful guardians.
.6 While Jeremiah was still weeping for the people, they brought him out with the people and dragged them into Babylon.
.7 But Baruch put dust on his head and sat and wailed this lamentation, saying:
Why has Jerusalem been devastated? Because of the sins of the beloved people she was delivered into the hands of enemies—because of our
.8 sins and those of the people. But let not the lawless ones boast and say:
"We were strong enough to take the city of God by our might;"
.9 but it was delivered to you because of our sins. And God will pity us and cause us to return to our city, but you will not survive!
.10 Blessed are our fathers, Abraham, Isaac and Jacob, for they departed from this world and did not see the destruction of this city.
.11 When he had said this, Baruch departed from the city, weeping and saying:
Grieving because of you, Jerusalem, I went out from you.
.12 And he remained sitting in a tomb, while the angels came to him and explained to him everything that the Lord revealed to him through them.

4.1 the city Ceth: + of Jerusalem ABarm P: Jerusalem hist
.6 the textual situation here is extremely confused and syntactically difficult; the ET is closest to eth
.8 by our might ABarm P: + you were not able to prevail against it C (cf eth)
.11 Grieving cf Ceth: om ABarm P
.11 I went out from you ABarm P: and he went out of the city Ceth (cf hist)
.12 that the Lord—them AB (cf arm) P: om Ceth

5.1   Ὁ δὲ Ἀβιμέλεχ ἤνεγκε τὰ σῦκα τῷ καύματι, καὶ καταλαβὼν
.2   δένδρον, ἐκάθισεν ὑπὸ τὴν σκιὰν αὐτοῦ τοῦ ἀναπαῆναι ὀλίγον.
       Καὶ κλίνας τὴν κεφαλὴν αὐτοῦ
       ἐπὶ τὸν κόφινον τῶν σύκων ὕπνωσεν κοιμώμενος ἔτη ἑξηκονταέξ·
       καὶ
.3   οὐκ ἐξυπνίσθη ἐκ τοῦ ὕπνου αὐτοῦ. Καὶ μετὰ ταῦτα ἐγερθεὶς ἀπὸ
       τοῦ ὕπνου αὐτοῦ, εἶπεν ὅτι,
       Ἡδέως ἐκοιμήθην ὀλίγον, ἀλλὰ βεβαρημένη ἐστὶν ἡ κεφαλή μου,
       ὅτι οὐκ ἐκορέσθην τοῦ ὕπνου μου.
.4   Εἶτα ἀνακαλύψας τὸν κόφινον τῶν σύκων, εὗρεν αὐτὰ στάζοντα
       γάλα.
.5   Καὶ εἶπεν·
       Ἤθελον κοιμηθῆναι ἔτι ὀλίγον, ὅτι βεβαρημένη ἐστὶν ἡ
          κεφαλή μου·
       ἀλλὰ φοβοῦμαι, μήπως κοιμηθῶ καὶ βραδυνῶ τοῦ ἐξυπνισθῆναι,
       καὶ ὀλιγωρήσῃ Ἰερεμίας ὁ πατήρ μου· εἰ μὴ γὰρ
       ἐσπούδαζεν, οὐκ ἂν ἀπέστειλέ με ὀρθροῦ σήμερον.
.6   Ἀναστὰς οὖν πορεύσομαι τῷ καύματι· οὐ γὰρ
       καῦμα οὐ κόπος ἐστὶ καθ' ἡμέραν;
.7   Ἐγερθεὶς οὖν ᾖρε τὸν κόφινον τῶν σύκων, καὶ ἐπέθηκεν ἐπὶ τῶν
       ὤμων αὐτοῦ·
       καὶ εἰσῆλθεν εἰς Ἰερουσαλήμ, καὶ οὐκ ἐπέγνω αὐτήν, οὔτε τὴν
       οἰκίαν οὔτε τὸν τόπον ἑαυτοῦ, οὔτε τὸ γένος ἑαυτοῦ οὔτέ
.8   τινα τῶν γνωρίμων εὗρεν. Καὶ εἶπεν·
       Εὐλογητὸς κύριος, ὅτι μεγάλη ἔκστασις ἐπέπεσεν ἐπ' ἐμὲ
       σήμερον.
.9   Οὐκ ἔστιν αὕτη ἡ πόλις Ἰερουσαλήμ· πεπλάνημαι τὴν ὁδόν,
       ὅτι διὰ τῆς ὁδοῦ τοῦ ὄρους ἦλθον, ἐγερθεὶς ἀπὸ
       τοῦ ὕπνου μου· καὶ βαρείας οὔσης τῆς κεφαλῆς μου διὰ τὸ μὴ
          κορεσθῆναί με
.10   τοῦ ὕπνου πεπλάνημαι τὴν ὁδόν. Θαυμαστὸν εἰπεῖν τοῦτο
       ἐναντίον
       Ἰερεμίου, ὅτι πεπλάνημαι τὴν ὁδόν.
.11   Ἐξῆλθε δὲ ἀπὸ τῆς πόλεως· καὶ κατανοήσας εἶδε τὰ σημεῖα
       τῆς πόλεως, καὶ εἶπεν·
       Αὕτη μὲν ἔστιν ἡ πόλις, πεπλάνημαι δέ τὴν ὁδόν.
.12   Καὶ πάλιν ὑπέστρεψεν εἰς τὴν πόλιν, καὶ ἐζήτησε, καὶ οὐδένα
       εὗρε
       τῶν ἰδίων, καὶ εἶπεν·
       Εὐλογητὸς κύριος, ὅτι μεγάλη ἔκστασις ἐπέπεσεν ἐπ' ἐμέ.
.13   Καὶ πάλιν ἐξῆλθεν ἔξω τῆς πόλεως, καὶ ἔμεινε λυπούμενος,
       μὴ εἰδὼς ποῦ ἀπέλθῃ.

5.1-13

5.1 But Abimelech took the figs in the burning heat; and coming upon
.2 a tree, he sat under its shade to rest a bit. And leaning his head on the basket of figs, he fell asleep and slept for 66 years; and he
.3 was not awakened from his slumber. And afterward, when he awoke from his sleep, he said:
I slept sweetly for a little while, but my head is heavy because I did not get enough sleep.
.4 Then he uncovered the basket of figs and found them dripping milk.
.5 And he said:
I would like to sleep a little longer, because my head is heavy. But I am afraid that I might fall asleep and be late in awakening and my father Jeremiah would think badly of me; for if he were
.6 not in a hurry, he would not have sent me today at daybreak. So I will get up, and proceed in the burning heat; for isn't there heat, isn't there toil every day?
.7 So he got up and took the basket of figs and placed it on his shoulders, and he entered into Jerusalem and did not recognize it—neither his own house, nor the place—nor did he find his own family or any of
.8 his acquaintances. And he said:
The Lord be blessed, for a great trance has come over me today!
.9 This is not the city Jerusalem—and I have lost my way because I came by the mountain road when I arose from my sleep; and since my head was heavy because I did not get
.10 enough sleep, I lost my way. It will seem incredible to Jeremiah that I lost my way!
.11 And he departed from the city; and as he searched he saw the landmarks of the city, and he said:
Indeed, this is the city; I lost my way.
.12 And again he returned to the city and searched, and found no one of his own people; and he said:
The Lord be blessed, for a great trance has come over me!
.13 And again he departed from the city, and he stayed there grieving, not knowing where he should go.

5.2 slumber arm Ceth: + according to God's command through the word which he spoke to Jeremiah I will hide him (+ in the shadow of the mountain P) AB P (cf hist) [see 3.14]
.3 awoke arm C hist: arose AB P: arose and awoke eth [see 5.9, 24]
.5 at daybreak Ceth: om AB (arm om context) P
.7 nor the place—acquaintances ABarm P (with slight variations) (cf hist): nor his own family/race C: om eth
.9 Jerusalem P eth (cf hist): om ABarm C
.9 when I arose from my sleep AB P c: om arm eth [see 5.3, 24]
.13 city arm Ceth (cf hist): + and he said Indeed these are the landmarks of the city (P adds more) AB (P)

.14   Καὶ ἀπέθηκε τὸν κόφινον, λέγων˙
            Καθέζομαι ὧδε ἕως ὁ κύριος ἄρῃ τὴν ἔκστασιν ταύτην ἀπ' ἐμοῦ.
.15   Καθημένου δὲ αὐτοῦ, εἶδέ τινα γηραιὸν ἐρχόμενον ἐξ ἀγροῦ, καὶ
      λέγει αὐτῷ 'Αβιμέλεχ˙
            Σοὶ λέγω, πρεσβῦτα, ποία ἐστὶν ἡ πόλις αὕτη;
.16   Καὶ εἶπεν αὐτῷ˙
            'Ιερουσαλήμ ἐστι.
.17   Καὶ λέγει αὐτῷ 'Αβιμέλεχ˙
            Ποῦ ἐστιν ὁ 'Ιερεμίας ὁ ἱερεὺς, καὶ Βαροὺχ ὁ ἀναγνώστης,
            καὶ πᾶς
            ὁ λαὸς τῆς πόλεως ταύτης, ὅτι οὐχ εὗρον αὐτούς;
.18   Καὶ εἶπεν αὐτῷ ὁ πρεσβύτης˙
            Οὐκ εἶ σὺ ἐκ τῆς πόλεως ταύτης, σήμερον μνησθεὶς τοῦ
            'Ιερεμίου,
            ὅτι ἐπερωτᾷς περὶ αὐτοῦ μετὰ τοσοῦτον χρόνον;
.19   'Ιερεμίας γὰρ ἐν Βαβυλῶνί ἐστι μετὰ τοῦ λαοῦ˙
            ᾐχμαλωτεύθησαν γὰρ ὑπὸ Ναβουχοδονόσορ τοῦ βασιλέως, καὶ
            μετ' αὐτῶν ἐστιν
            'Ιερεμίας εὐαγγελίσασθαι αὐτοῖς καὶ κατηχῆσαι αὐτοὺς
            τὸν λόγον.
.20   Εὐθὺς δὲ ἀκούσας 'Αβιμέλεχ παρὰ τοῦ γηραιοῦ ἀνθρώπου, εἶπεν˙
            Εἰ μὴ ἦς πρεσβύτης, καὶ ὅτι
            οὐκ ἐξὸν ἀνθρώπῳ ὑβρίσαι τὸν μείζονα αὐτοῦ,
            ἐπικατεγέλων ἄν σοι καὶ ἔλεγον ὅτι μαίνῃ˙
            ὅτι εἶπας, 'Ηχμαλωτεύθη ὁ λαὸς εἰς
.21   Βαβυλῶνα. Εἰ ἦσαν οἱ καταρράκται τοῦ οὐρανοῦ κατελθόντες
            ἐπ' αὐτούς,
            οὔπω ἐστὶ καιρὸς ἀπελθεῖν εἰς Βαβυλῶνα.
.22   Πόση γὰρ ὥρα ἐστὶν, ἀφ' οὗ ἀπέστειλέ με ὁ πατήρ μου
            'Ιερεμίας εἰς
            τὸ χωρίον τοῦ 'Αγρίππα ἐνέγκαι ὀλίγα σῦκα, ἵνα δίδωμεν
.23   τοῖς νοσοῦσι τοῦ λαοῦ; Καὶ ἀπελθὼν ἤνεγκον αὐτὰ, καὶ
      ἐλθὼν ἐπί τι δένδρον τῷ καύματι, ἐκάθισα τοῦ ἀναπαῆναι
      ὀλίγον, καὶ ἔκλινα τὴν κεφαλήν μου ἐπὶ τὸν κόφινον, καὶ
      ἐκοιμήθην.
.24   Καὶ ἐξυπνισθεὶς ἀπεκάλυψα τὸν κόφινον τῶν σύκων, νομίζων
      ὅτι
      ἐβράδυνα, καὶ εὗρον τὰ σῦκα στάζοντα γάλα, καθὼς
.25   συνέλεξα αὐτά. Σὺ δὲ λέγεις, ὅτι ᾐχμαλωτεύθη ὁ λαὸς
.26   εἰς Βαβυλῶνα. Ἵνα δὲ γνῷς, λάβε,   ἴδε τὰ σῦκα.

THE THINGS OMITTED FROM JEREMIAH

5.14-26

5.14   And he put down the basket, saying:
    I will sit here until the Lord takes this trance from me.

.15   And as he sat, he saw an old man coming from the field; and Abimelech said to him:
    I say to you, old man, what city is this?

.16   And he said to him:
    It is Jerusalem.

.17   And Abimelech said to him:
    Where is Jeremiah the priest, and Baruch the secretary, and all the people of this city, for I could not find them?

.18   And the old man said to him:
    Are you not from this city, seeing that you remember Jeremiah today, because you are asking about him after such a long time?

.19   For Jeremiah is in Babylon with the people; for they were taken captive by king Nebuchadnezzar, and Jeremiah is with them to preach the good news to them and to teach them the word.

.20   As soon as Abimelech heard this from the old man, he said:
    If you were not an old man, and if it were not for the fact that it is not lawful for a man to upbraid one older than himself, I would laugh at you and say that you are out of your mind—since you say that the people have been taken captive into

.21   Babylon. Even if the heavenly torrents had descended on them,

.22   there has not yet been time for them to go into Babylon! For how much time has passed since my father Jeremiah sent me to the estate of Agrippa to bring a few figs, so that I might give

.23   them to the sick among the people? And I went and got them, and when I came to a certain tree in the burning heat, I sat to rest a little; and I leaned my head on the basket and fell asleep.

.24   And when I awoke I uncovered the basket of figs, supposing that I was late; and I found the figs dripping milk, just as I had

.25   collected them. But you claim that the people have been taken

.26   captive into Babylon. But that you might know, take the figs and see!

5.17   priest arm eth: high priest C: priest of God AB hist: high priest of God P
.18   to him ceth (cf hist): to Abimelech ABarm P
.19   king ABarm: of the Chaldeans P: of Babylon C: of Persia eth
.20   for a man cf Ceth: + of God ABarm P
.22   so that I might give them to AB P (cf eth hist): for arm C
.25   that AB P Ceth: + in that space of time arm hist

5.27-6.5a

.27 Καὶ ἀνεκάλυψε τὸν κόφινον τῶν σύκων τῷ γέροντι, καὶ εἶδεν αὐτὰ
.28 στάζοντα γάλα. Ἰδὼν δὲ αὐτὰ ὁ γηραιὸς ἄνθρωπος, εἶπεν·
Ὦ υἱέ μου, δίκαιος ἄνθρωπος εἶ σὺ, καὶ οὐκ ἠθέλησεν ὁ θεὸς
Ἡ ἰδεῖν σε τὴν ἐρήμωσιν τῆς πόλεως· ἤνεγκε γὰρ ταύτην τὴν ἔκστασιν ἐπὶ
.29 σὲ. Ἰδοὺ γὰρ ἐξήκοντα καὶ ἓξ ἔτη σήμερόν εἰσιν ἀφ' οὗ ἠχμαλωτεύθη ὁ λαὸς
.30 εἰς Βαβυλῶνα. Καὶ ἵνα μάθῃς, τέκνον,
ὅτι ἀληθές ἐστιν ἅπερ λέγω σοι ἀνάβλεψον εἰς τὸν ἀγρὸν καὶ ἴδε,
.31 ὅτι οὐκ ἔστι ἐφάνη ἡ αὔξησις τῶν γενημάτων. Ἴδε καὶ τὰ σῦκα, ὅτι καιρὸς αὐτῶν οὐκ ἔστι, καὶ γνῶθι.
.32 Τότε ἔκραξε μεγάλῃ φωνῇ Ἀβιμέλεχ, λέγων·
Εὐλογήσω σε, ὁ θεὸς τοῦ οὐρανοῦ καὶ τῆς γῆς, ἡ ἀνάπαυσις τῶν ψυχῶν
τῶν δικαίων ἐν παντὶ τόπῳ.
.33 Εἶτα λέγει τῷ γηραιῷ ἀνθρώπῳ·
Ποῖός ἐστιν ὁ μὴν οὗτος;
.34 Ὁ δὲ εἶπε·
Νισσάν, ὅ ἐστιν Ἀβιβ.
.35 Καὶ ἐπάρας ἐκ τῶν σύκων, ἔδωκε τῷ γηραιῷ ἀνθρώπῳ, καὶ λέγει αὐτῷ·
Ὁ θεὸς φωταγωγήσει σε εἰς τὴν ἄνω πόλιν Ἰερουσαλήμ.
6.1 Μετὰ ταῦτα ἐξῆλθεν Ἀβιμέλεχ ἔξω τῆς πόλεως, καὶ προσηύξατο πρὸς κύριον.
.2 Καὶ ἰδοὺ ἄγγελος κυρίου ἦλθε, καὶ κρατήσας αὐτοῦ τῆς δεξίας χειρὸς
ἀπεκατέστησεν αὐτὸν εἰς τὸν τόπον ὅπου ἦν Βαροὺχ καθεζόμενος· εὗρε δὲ αὐτὸν ἐν
.3 μνημείῳ. Καὶ ἐν τῷ θεωρῆσαι ἀλλήλους, ἔκλαυσαν ἀμφότεροι καὶ κατεφίλησαν ἀλλήλους.
.4 Ἀναβλέψας δὲ Βαροὺχ τοῖς ὀφθαλμοῖς αὐτοῦ εἶδε τὰ σῦκα
.5 ἐσκεπασμένα ἐν τῷ κοφίνῳ τοῦ Ἀβιμελεχ. Καὶ ἄρας τοὺς ὀφθαλμοὺς αὐτοῦ εἰς
τὸν οὐρανὸν, προσηύξατο λέγων·

5.27-6:5a

5.27 And he uncovered the basket of figs for the old man, and he saw them
.28 dripping milk. And when the old man saw them, he said:
O my son, you are a righteous man, and God did not want you to see the desolation of the city, so he brought this trance upon
.29 you. For behold, it is 66 years today since the people were
.30 taken captive into Babylon. But that you might learn, my son, that what I tell you is true—look into the field and see
.31 that the ripening of the crops has not appeared. And notice that the figs are not in season, and be enlightened.
.32 Then Abimelech cried out in a loud voice, saying:
I bless you, God of heaven and earth, the Rest of the souls of the righteous in every place!
.33 Then he said to the old man:
What month is this?
.34 And he said:
Nisan (which is Abib).
.35 And taking some of the figs, he gave them to the old man and said to him:
May God illumine your way to the city above, Jerusalem.

6.1 After this, Abimelech went out of the city and prayed to the Lord.
.2 And behold, an angel of the Lord came and took him by the right hand and brought him back to where Baruch was sitting, and he found him in
.3 a tomb. And when they saw each other, they both went and kissed each
.4 other. But when Baruch looked up he saw with his own eyes the figs
.5 that were covered in Abimelech's basket. And lifting his eyes to heaven, he prayed, saying:

5.28 righteous man Ceth: son of a righteous man ABarm P hist
.28 he arm P C (cf hist): God AB (eth?)
.29 today P Ceth: om ABarm
.30 what I tell you ABarm P: it Ceth
.32 God ABarm P: Lord God Ceth
.32 every place ABarm P eth: + the true light [see 9.3] the true paymaster who is great awesome forever amen C
.34 which is Abib cj [$\overline{IB}$ = 12]: which is 12th AB: the first month arm: which is April the 12th day P: which is Miyazya the 12th (day) eth: C seems unintelligible as it stands

6.2 and took him by the right hand ABarm P: om Ceth
.4 Abimelech's ABarm P: the Ceth

6.5b-17

.6 Σὺ ὁ θεὸς ὁ παρέχων μισθαποδοσίαν τοῖς ἀγάπωσί σε.
Ἑτοίμασον
σεαυτὴν, ἡ καρδία μου, καὶ εὐφραίνου, καὶ ἀγάλλου ἐν τῷ
σκηνώματί σου λέγων τῷ σαρκίκῳ οἴκῳ σου τὸ πένθος σου
μετεστράφη εἰς χαράν· "ἔρχεται γὰρ ὁ ἱκανὸς, καὶ ἀρεῖ
σε ἐν τῷ σκηνώματί σου, οὐ γὰρ γέγονέ σοι ἁμαρτία.
.7 Ἀνάψυξον ἐν τῷ σκηνώματί σου ἐν τῇ παρθενικῇ σου πίστει
καὶ πίστευσον
.8 ὅτι ζήσεις. Ἐπίβλεψον ἐπὶ τὸν κόφινον τοῦτον τῶν σύκων·
ἰδοὺ γὰρ
ἐξηκονταὲξ ἔτη ἐποίησαν, καὶ οὐκ ἐμαράνθησαν, οὐδὲ ὤζεσαν,
.9 ἀλλὰ στάζουσι τοῦ γάλακτος. Οὕτως γίνεταί σοι ἡ σάρξ μου,
ἐὰν ποιήσῃς τὰ προσταχθέντα σου ὑπὸ τοῦ ἀγγέλου τῆς
δικαιοσύνης.
.10 Ὁ φυλάξας τὸν κόφινον τῶν σύκων, αὐτὸς πάλιν
φυλάξει σε ἐν τῇ δυνάμει αὐτοῦ.
.11 Ταῦτα εἰπὼν ὁ Βαροὺχ, λέγει τῷ Ἀβιμέλεχ·
Ἀνάστηθι, καὶ εὐξώμεθα, ἵνα γνωρίσῃ ἡμῖν ὁ κύριος
πῶς δυνησώμεθα ἀποστεῖλαι τὴν φάσιν τῷ Ἱερεμίᾳ εἰς
Βαβυλῶνα
διὰ τὴν σκέπην τὴν γενομένην σοι ἐν τῇ ὁδῷ.
.12 Καὶ ἤρξατο Βαροὺχ, λέγων·
Ἡ δύναμις ἡμῶν, ὁ θεὸς κύριε, τὸ ἐκλεκτὸν φῶς, τὸ ἐξελθὸν
.13 ἐκ στόματός σου. Παρακαλοῦμεν καὶ δεόμεθά σου τῆς
ἀγαθότητος,
τὸ μέγα ὄνομα, ὃ οὐδεὶς δύναται γνῶναι, ἄκουσον τῆς φωνῆς
.14 τῶν δούλων σου, καὶ γενοῦ γνῶσις ἐν τῇ καρδίᾳ ἡμῶν. Τί
ποιήσωμεν, καὶ πῶς ἀποστείλωμεν πρὸς Ἱερεμίαν εἰς
Βαβυλῶνα τὴν φάσιν ταύτην;
.15 Ἔτι δὲ προσευχομένου τοῦ Βαροὺχ, ἰδοὺ ἄγγελος κυρίου
ἦλθε, καὶ λέγει τῷ Βαροὺχ ἅπαντας τοὺς λόγους τούτους·
Ὁ σύμβουλος τοῦ φωτὸς, μὴ μεριμνήσῃς τὸ πῶς ἀποστείλῃς
πρὸς Ἱερεμίαν· ἔρχεται γὰρ πρός σε ὥρᾳ τοῦ φωτὸς αὔριον
ἀετός,
καὶ σὺ ἐπισκέψῃ πρὸς Ἱερεμίαν.
.16 Γράψον οὖν ἐν τῇ ἐπιστολῇ ὅτι,
Λάλησον τοῖς υἱοῖς Ἰσραὴλ· Ὁ γενόμενος
ἐν ὑμῖν ξένος, ἀφορισθήτω, καὶ ποιήσωσι ιέ ἡμέρας·
καὶ μετὰ ταῦτα εἰσάξω ὑμᾶς εἰς
.17 τὴν πόλιν ὑμῶν, λέγει κύριος. Ὁ μὴ ἀφοριζόμενος ἐκ
τῆς Βαβυλῶνος, οὐ μὴ εἰσέλθῃ εἰς τὴν πόλιν· καὶ
ἐπιτιμῶ αὐτοῖς, τοῦ μὴ ἀποδεχθῆναι αὐτοὺς
αὖθις ὑπὸ τῶν Βαβυλωνιτῶν, λέγει κύριος.

6.6	You are the God who gives a reward to those who love you. Prepare yourself, my heart, and rejoice and be glad while you are in your tabernacle, saying to your fleshly house, "your grief has been changed to joy;" for the Sufficient One is coming and will deliver you in your tabernacle—for there is no sin in you.
.7	Revive in your tabernacle, in your virginal faith, and believe
.8	that you will live! Look at this basket of figs—for behold, they are 66 years old and have not become shrivelled or rotten,
.9	but they are dripping milk. So it will be with you, my flesh, if you do what is commanded you by the angel of righteousness.
.10	He who preserved the basket of figs, the same will again preserve you by his power.
.11	When Baruch had said this, he said to Abimelech: Stand up and let us pray that the Lord may make known to us how we shall be able to send to Jeremiah in Babylon the report about the shelter provided for you on the way.
.12	And Baruch prayed, saying: Lord God, our strength is the elect light which comes forth
.13	from your mouth. We beseech and beg of your goodness—you whose great name no one is able to know—hear the voice
.14	of your servants and let knowledge come into our hearts. What shall we do, and how shall we send this report to Jeremiah in Babylon?
.15	And while Baruch was still praying, behold an angel of the Lord came and said all these words to Baruch: Agent of the light, do not be anxious about how you will send to Jeremiah; for an eagle is coming to you at the hour of
.16	light tomorrow, and you will direct him to Jeremiah. Therefore, write in a letter: Say to the children of Israel: Let the stranger who comes among you be set apart and let 15 days go by; and after this I will lead you into your
.17	city, says the Lord. He who is not separated from Babylon will not enter into the city; and I will punish them by keeping them from being received back by the Babylonians, says the Lord.

6.5	those who love you ABarm: those who fear you in truth P (along with other similar expansions): to his saints C: to his righteous eth
.6	fleshly house AB (cf arm) P: holy house of flesh (?) Ceth
.6b	in your tabernacle Ceth: from your tabernacle ABarm P
.7	faith arm Ceth: flock (of sheep) AB P
.12-.14	Ceth have the singular, not plural, throughout the prayer
.12	Baruch Ceth: + and Abimelech ABarm P
.14	this report ABarm P: om Ceth
.15	Baruch was C: he was eth: Baruch and Abimelech were AB P: arm lacks context
.15	all these words ABarm P: om Ceth

6.18-7.4

.18/ Καὶ ταῦτα εἰπὼν ὁ ἄγγελος, ἀπῆλθεν ἀπὸ τοῦ Βαρούχ. Ὁ δὲ
.19 Βαροὺχ
     ἀπέστειλεν εἰς τὴν ἀγορὰν τῶν ἐθνῶν καὶ ἤνεγκε χάρτην καὶ
        μέλανα, καὶ ἔγραψεν
     ἐπιστολὴν περιέχουσαν οὕτως·
        Βαροὺχ ὁ δοῦλος τοῦ θεοῦ γράφει τῷ Ἰερεμίᾳ ἐν τῇ
           αἰχμαλωσίᾳ
        τῆς Βαβυλῶνος·
.20   Χαῖρε καὶ ἀγαλλιῶ, ὅτι ὁ θεὸς οὐκ ἀφῆκεν ἡμᾶς ἐξελθεῖν ἐκ
     τοῦ σώματος τούτου λυπουμένους διὰ τὴν πόλιν τὴν ἐρημωθεῖ-
        σαν καὶ ὑβρισθεῖσαν.
.21 Διὰ τοῦτο ἐσπλαγχνίσθη ὁ κύριος ἐπὶ τῶν δακρύων ἡμῶν,
        καὶ ἐμνήσθη
     τῆς διαθήκης, ἧς ἔστησε μετὰ τῶν πατέρων ἡμῶν Ἀβραάμ,
        Ἰσαὰκ,
.22 καὶ Ἰακώβ. Καὶ ἀπέστειλε πρός με τὸν ἄγγελον αὐτοῦ, καὶ
     εἶπέ μοι τοὺς λόγους
.23 τούτους, οὓς ἀπέστειλα πρός σε. Οὗτοι οὖν εἰσιν οἱ
        λόγοι, οὓς
     εἶπε κύριος ὁ θεὸς Ἰσραήλ, ὁ ἐξαγαγὼν ἡμᾶς ἐκ γῆς
        Αἰγύπτου, ἐκ τῆς
     μεγάλης καμίνου·
        Ὅτι οὐκ ἐφυλάξατε τὰ δικαιώματά μου, ἀλλὰ
        ὑψώθη ἡ καρδία ὑμῶν, καὶ ἐτραχηλιάσατε ἐνώπιόν μου,
           ἐν ὀργῇ καὶ
.24 θυμῷ παρέδωκα ὑμᾶς τῇ καμίνῳ εἰς Βαβυλῶνα. Ἐὰν
     οὖν ἀκούσητε τῆς φωνῆς μου, λέγει κύριος, ἐκ
     στόματος Ἰερεμίου τοῦ παιδός μου, ὁ ἀκούων, ἀναφέρω
        αὐτὸν
     ἐκ τῆς Βαβυλῶνος· ὁ δὲ μὴ ἀκούων,
     ξένος γενήσεται τῆς Ἰερουσαλὴμ καὶ τῆς Βαβυλῶνος.
.25 Δοκιμάσεις δὲ αὐτοὺς ἐκ τοῦ ὕδατος τοῦ Ἰορδάνου·
     ὁ μὴ ἀκούων φανερὸς γενήσεται· τοῦτο τὸ σημεῖόν ἐστι
        τῆς
     μεγάλης σφραγῖδος.

6.18-.25

6.18/
.19 And when the angel had said this, he departed from Baruch. And Baruch sent to the market of the gentiles and got papyrus and ink and wrote a letter as follows:

Baruch, the servant of God, writes to Jeremiah in the captivity of Babylon:

.20 Greetings! Rejoice, for God has not allowed us to depart from this
.21 body grieving for the city which was laid waste and outraged. Wherefore the Lord has had compassion on our tears, and has remembered the covenant which he established with our fathers Abraham, Isaac
.22 and Jacob. And he sent his angel to me, and he told me these words
.23 which I send to you. These, then, are the words which the Lord, the God of Israel, spoke, who led us out of Egypt, out of the great furnace:

Because you did not keep my ordinances, but your heart was lifted up, and you were haughty before me, in anger and
.24 wrath I delivered you to the furnace in Babylon. If, therefore, says the Lord, you listen to my voice, from the mouth of Jeremiah my servant, I will bring the one who listens up from Babylon; but the one who does not listen will become a stranger to Jerusalem and to Babylon.
.25 And you will test them by means of the water of the Jordan; whoever does not listen will be exposed—this is the sign of the great seal.

6.19 market Ceth: dispersed ABarm P
 .24 and to Babylon C (cf eth): om ABarm P
 .25 You will P Ceth: I will ABarm

7.1 Καὶ ἀνέστη Βαροὺχ, καὶ ἐξῆλθεν ἐκ τοῦ μνημείου καὶ
     εὗρεν τὸν ἀετὸν
.2   καθεζόμενον ἐκτὸς τοῦ μνημείου. Καὶ ἀποκριθεὶς ἀνθρωπίνῃ
     φωνῇ εἶπεν αὐτῷ ὁ ἀετός·
     Χαῖρε, Βαροὺχ, ὁ οἰκονόμος τῆς πίστεως.
.3   Καὶ εἶπεν αὐτῷ Βαροὺχ ὅτι,
     Ἐκλεκτός εἶ σὺ ὁ λαλῶν ἐκ πάντων τῶν πετεινῶν τοῦ
     οὐρανοῦ,
     ἐκ τῆς γὰρ αὐγῆς τῶν ὀφθαλμῶν σου δῆλόν ἐστι· δεῖξον
     μοι οὖν, τί ποιεῖς
     ἐνταῦθα;
.4   Καὶ εἶπεν αὐτῷ ὁ ἀετός·
     Ἀπεστάλην ὧδε, ὅπως πᾶσαν φάσιν ἣν θέλεις, ἀποστείλῃς
     δι' ἐμοῦ.

7.1-.4

7.1 And Baruch got up and departed from the tomb and found the eagle
.2 sitting outside the tomb. And the eagle said to him in a human voice:
Hail, Baruch, steward of the faith.
.3 And Baruch said to him:
You who speak are chosen from among all the birds of heaven, for this is clear from the gleam of your eyes; tell me, then, what are you doing here?
.4 And the eagle said to him:
I was sent here so that you might through me send whatever message you want.

7.1 and found—tomb P C (cf arm): om AB: when he had thus written eth
.4 I was sent AB eth: + by the Lord P: the Lord sent me arm: God sent me C

7.5-16
.5 Καὶ εἶπεν αὐτῷ Βαρούχ·
Εἰ δύνασαι σὺ ἐπᾶραι τὴν φάσιν ταύτην τῷ Ἰερεμίᾳ εἰς Βαβυλῶνα;
.6 Καὶ εἶπεν αὐτῷ ὁ ἀετός·
Εἰς τοῦτο γὰρ καὶ ἀπεστάλην.
.7 Καὶ ἄρας Βαροὺχ τὴν ἐπιστολήν, καὶ δεκαπέντε σῦκα ἐκ τοῦ κοφίνου τοῦ Ἀβιμέλεχ,
ἔδησεν αὐτὰ εἰς τὸν τράχηλον τοῦ ἀετοῦ, καὶ εἶπεν αὐτῷ·
Σοὶ λέγω, βασιλεῦ τῶν πετεινῶν, ἄπελθε ἐν εἰρήνῃ μεθ' ὑγείας, καὶ
.8 τὴν φάσιν ἔνεγκόν μοι. Μὴ ὁμοιωθῇς τῷ κόρακι, ὃν ἐξαπέστειλε Νῶε
καὶ οὐκ ἀπεστράφη ἔτι πρὸς αὐτὸν εἰς τὴν κιβωτόν· ἀλλὰ
ὁμοιώθητι τῇ περιστερᾷ, ἥτις ἐκ τρίτου φάσιν ἤνεγκε
.9 τῷ δικαίῳ. Οὕτως καὶ σύ, ἆρον τὴν καλὴν φάσιν ταύτην τῷ Ἰερεμίᾳ
καὶ τοῖς σὺν αὐτῷ δεσμίοις ἵνα εὖ σοι γένηται,
ἆρον τὸν χάρτην τοῦτον τῷ λαῷ καὶ τῷ ἐκλεκτῷ τοῦ θεοῦ.
.10 Ἐὰν κυκλώσωσί σε πάντα τὰ πετεινὰ τοῦ οὐρανοῦ, καὶ βούλωνται πολεμῆσαι
.11 μετὰ σοῦ, ἀγώνισαι· ὁ κύριος δώῃ σοι δύναμιν. Καὶ μὴ
ἐκκλίνῃς εἰς τὰ δεξιά, μήτε εἰς τὰ ἀριστερά, ἀλλ'
ὡς βέλος ὕπαγον ὀρθῶς, ἄπελθε ἐν τῇ δυνάμει τοῦ θεοῦ, καὶ ἔσται ἡ δόξα
κυρίου μετὰ σοῦ ἐν πάσῃ τῇ ὁδῷ ᾗ πορεύσῃ.
.12 Τότε ὁ ἀετὸς ἐπετάσθη, ἔχων τὴν ἐπιστολὴν ἐν τῷ τραχήλῳ αὐτοῦ, καὶ ἀπῆλθεν
εἰς Βαβυλῶνα καὶ ἐλθὼν ἀνεπαύσατο ἐπί τι ξύλον ἔξω τῆς πόλεως εἰς
.13 τόπον ἔρημον. Ἐσιώπησε δὲ ἕως οὗ διῆλθεν Ἰερεμίας, αὐτὸς γὰρ καὶ
ἄλλοι τινὲς τοῦ λαοῦ ἐξήρχοντο θάψαι νεκρὸν ἔξω τῆς πόλεως.
.14 Ἠτήσατο γὰρ Ἰερεμίας παρὰ τοῦ βασιλέως Ναβουχοδονόσορ, λέγων·
Δός μοι τόπον ποῦ θάψω τοὺς νεκροὺς τοῦ λαοῦ μου·
καὶ ἔδωκεν αὐτῷ ὁ βασιλεύς.
.15 Ἀπερχομένων δὲ αὐτῶν καὶ κλαιόντων μετὰ τοῦ νεκροῦ, ἦλθον
.16 κατέναντι τοῦ ἀετοῦ. Καὶ ἔκραξεν ὁ ἀετός, μεγάλῃ φωνῇ λέγων·
Σοὶ λέγω, Ἰερεμία ὁ ἐκλεκτὸς τοῦ θεοῦ, ἄπελθε, σύναξον
τὸν λαὸν καὶ ἐλθὲ ἐνταῦθα ἵνα ἀκούσωσι
ἐπιστολῆς ἧς ἤνεγκά σοι ἀπὸ τοῦ Βαροὺχ καὶ τοῦ Ἀβιμέλεχ.

7.5-16

7.5 And Baruch said to him:
Can you carry this message to Jeremiah in Babylon?
.6 And the eagle said to him:
Indeed, it was for this reason I was sent.
.7 And Baruch took the letter, and 15 figs from Abimelech's basket, and tied them to the eagle's neck and said to him:
I say to you, king of the birds, go in peace with good health and
.8 carry the message for me. Do not be like the raven which Noah sent out and which never came back to him in the ark; but be like the dove which, the third time, brought a report to the
.9 righteous one. So you also, take this good message to Jeremiah and to those in bondage with him, that it may be well with you—take this papyrus to the people and to the chosen one of God.
.10 Even if all the birds of heaven surround you and want to fight
.11 with you, struggle—the Lord will give you strength. And do not turn aside to the right or to the left, but straight as a speeding arrow, go in the power of God, and the glory of the Lord will be with you the entire way.
.12 Then the eagle took flight and went away to Babylon, having the letter tied to his neck; and when he arrived he rested on a post outside the city in
.13 a desert place. And he kept silent until Jeremiah came along, for he and some of the people were coming out to bury a corpse outside the city.
.14 (For Jeremiah had petitioned king Nebuchadnezzar, saying: "Give me a place where I may bury those of my people who have died;" and the king gave it to him.)
.15 And as they were coming out with the body, and weeping, they came to
.16 where the eagle was. And the eagle cried out in a loud voice, saying:
I say to you, Jeremiah the chosen one of God, go and gather together the people and come here so that they may hear a letter which I have brought to you from Baruch and Abimelech.

7.11 and the glory—way ABarm P: om Ceth
.12 tied to his neck arm P C: om AB eth
.13 some of arm Ceth: om AB P
.14 the king ABarm P: he Ceth
.16 in a loud voice arm eth: in a human voice P: om AB C
.16 the people ABarm P: all the people Ceth
.16 a letter ABarm (cf P): the good proclamation (+ of God, C) (C) eth

7.17-23
.17 Ἀκούσας δὲ ὁ Ἰερεμίας, ἐδόξασε τὸν θεόν· καὶ ἀπελθὼν
συνῆξε τὸν λαὸν σὺν γυναιξὶ καὶ τέκνοις,
.18 καὶ ἦλθεν ὅπου ἦν ὁ ἀετός. Καὶ κατῆλθεν ὁ ἀετὸς ἐπὶ
.19 τὸν τεθνηκότα, καὶ ἀνέζησε. Γέγονε δὲ τοῦτο, ἵνα
.20 πιστεύσωσιν. Ἐθαύμασε δὲ πᾶς ὁ λαὸς ἐπὶ τῷ
γεγονότι, λέγοντες ὅτι,
Μὴ οὗτος ὁ θεὸς ὁ ὀφθεὶς τοῖς πατράσιν ἡμῶν ἐν τῇ ἐρήμῳ
διὰ Μωϋσέως, καὶ νῦν ἐφάνη ἡμῖν διὰ τοῦ ἀετοῦ τούτου;
.21 Καὶ εἶπεν ὁ ἀετός·
Σοὶ λέγω Ἰερεμία, δεῦρο λῦσον τὴν ἐπιστολὴν ταύτην, καὶ
ἀνάγνωθι αὐτὴν
τῷ λαῷ·
λύσας οὖν τὴν ἐπιστολὴν, ἀνέγνω αὐτὴν τῷ λαῷ.
.22 Καὶ ἀκούσας ὁ λαὸς ἔκλαυσαν καὶ ἐπέθηκαν χοῦν ἐπὶ τὰς κεφαλὰς
αὐτῶν,
καὶ ἔλεγον τῷ Ἰερεμίᾳ·
Σῶσον ἡμᾶς καὶ ἀπάγγειλον ἡμῖν τί ποιήσωμεν ἵνα εἰσέλθωμεν
πάλιν
εἰς τὴν πόλιν ἡμῶν.
.23 Ἀποκριθεὶς δὲ Ἰερεμίας εἶπεν αὐτοῖς·
Πάντα ὅσα ἐκ τῆς ἐπιστολῆς ἠκούσατε, φυλάξατε καὶ εἰσάξει
ἡμᾶς κύριος
εἰς τὴν πόλιν ἡμῶν.

7.17-23

7.17 And when Jeremiah heard this, he glorified God; and he went and gathered together the people along with their wives and children,
.18 and he came to where the eagle was. And the eagle came down on
.19 the corpse, and it revived. (Now this took place so that they
.20 might believe.) And all the people were astounded at what had happened, and said:
> This is the God who appeared to our fathers in the wilderness through Moses, and now he has appeared to us through this eagle.

.21 And the eagle said:
> I say to you, Jeremiah, come, untie this letter and read it to the people—

So he untied the letter and read it to the people.

.22 And when the people heard it, they wept and put dust on their heads, and they said to Jeremiah:
> Deliver us and tell us what to do that we may once again enter our city.

.23 And Jeremiah answered and said to them:
> Do whatever you heard from the letter, and the Lord will lead us into our city.

7.18 revived arm P Ceth: + and arose AB
.20 Moses ABarm P: + and he made himself into the form of an eagle Ceth
.21 through this eagle AB P: through this great eagle Ceth: om arm
.22 Deliver us and P C (cf eth): om ABarm
.23 Jeremiah answered and Ceth: he ABarm P
.23 from the letter Ceth: om ABarm P

7.24-31a

.24 Ἔγραψε δὲ καὶ ἐπιστολὴν ὁ Ἱερεμίας τῷ Βαροὺχ λέγων οὕτως·
Υἱέ μου ἀγαπητέ, μὴ ἀμελήσῃς ἐν ταῖς προσευχαῖς σου
δεόμενος τοῦ θεοῦ
ὑπὲρ ἡμῶν ὅπως κατευοδόσῃ τὴν ὁδὸν ἡμῶν ἄχρις ἂν ἐξέλθωμεν
ἐκ τῶν
.25 προσταγμάτων τοῦ ἀνόμου βασιλέως τούτου. Δίκαιος γὰρ
εὑρέθης
ἐνάντιον τοῦ θεοῦ, καὶ οὐκ ἔασέν σε εἰσελθεῖν ἐνταῦθα
ὅπως μὴ ἴδῃς τὴν κάκωσιν
τὴν γενομένην τῷ λαῷ ὑπὸ τῶν Βαβυλωνίων.
.26 Ὥσπερ γὰρ πατὴρ, υἱὸν μονογενῆ ἔχων, τούτου δὲ παραδοθέντος
εἰς τιμωρίαν· οἱ ἰδόντες τὸν πατέρα αὐτοῦ καὶ
παραμυθούμενοι αὐτὸν, σκέπουσιν
τὸ πρόσωπον αὐτοῦ, ἵνα μὴ ἴδῃ πῶς τιμωρεῖται αὐτὸς ὁ υἱὸς
καὶ πλείονα
.27 φθαρῇ ἀπὸ τῆς λύπης. Οὕτως γάρ σε ἐλέησεν ὁ θεὸς καὶ οὐκ
ἔασέν σε
.28 ἐλθεῖν εἰς Βαβυλῶνα ἵνα μὴ ἴδῃς τὴν κάκωσιν τοῦ λαοῦ.
Ἀφ' ἧς γὰρ
εἰσήλθομεν ἐνταῦθα οὐκ ἐπαύσατο ἡ λύπη ἀφ' ἡμῶν, ἑξήκοντα
καὶ ἓξ ἔτη σήμερον.
.29 Πολλάκις γὰρ ἐξερχόμενος ηὕρισκον ἐκ τοῦ λαοῦ κρεμαμένους
ὑπὸ
Ναβουχοδονόσορ βασιλέως, κλαίοντας καὶ λέγοντας·
Ἐλέησον ἡμᾶς, ὁ θεὸς Ζάρ.
.30 Ἀκούων ταῦτα, ἐλυπούμην καὶ ἔκλαιον δισσὸν κλαυθμόν,
οὐ μόνον
ὅτι ἐκρέμαντο, ἀλλ' ὅτι ἐπεκαλοῦντο θεὸν ἀλλότριον
.31 λέγοντες, Ἐλέησον ἡμᾶς. Ἐμνημόνευον δὲ ἡμέρας ἑορτῆς
ἃς ἐποιοῦμεν ἐν Ἱερουσαλὴμ πρὸ τοῦ ἡμᾶς αἰχμαλωτευθῆναι·

7.24-26 reads as follows in the (reconstructed) BAH arm (slav) text:

.24 Ἔγραψε δὲ Ἱερεμίας ἐπιστολὴν (+ εἰς Ἱερουσαλήμ BA)
πρὸς Βαροὺχ καὶ Ἀβιμέλεχ ἐνώπιον παντὸς τοῦ λαοῦ
(.25) τὰς θλίψεις τὰς γενόμενας εἰς αὐτούς,
τὸ πῶς παρελήφθησαν ὑπὸ τοῦ βασιλέως τῶν
(.26) Χαλδαίων καὶ τὸ πῶς ἕκαστος τὸν πατέρα αὐτοῦ
ἐθεώρει δεσμευόμενον καὶ πατὴρ τέκνον παραδόθεντα
εἰς τιμωρίαν. Οἱ δὲ θέλοντες παραμυθήσασθαι
τὸν πατέρα αὐτοῦ ἔσκεπον τὸ πρόσωπον αὐτοῦ
ἵνα μὴ ἴδῃ τὸν υἱὸν αὐτοῦ τιμωρούμενον.
Καὶ ὁ θεὸς ἐσκέπασέν σε καὶ Ἀβιμέλεχ
ἵνα μὴ ἴδητε ἡμᾶς τιμωρουμένους. . .

7.24-31a

7.24 And Jeremiah wrote a letter to Baruch, saying thus:
My beloved son, do not be negligent in your prayers, beseeching God on our behalf, that he might direct our way until we come out of the
.25 jurisdiction of this lawless king. For you have been found righteous before God, and he did not let you come here, lest you see the affliction which has come upon the people at the hands of the Babylonians.
.26 For it is like a father with an only son, who is given over for punishment; and those who see his father and console him cover his face, lest he see how his son is being punished, and be even more
.27 ravaged by grief. For thus God took pity on you and did not let you
.28 enter Babylon lest you see the affliction of the people. For since
.29 we came here, grief has not left us, for 66 years today. For many times when I went out I found some of the people hung up by king Nebuchadnezzar, crying and saying:
"Have mercy on us, God-ZAR!"
.30 When I heard this, I grieved and cried with two-fold mourning, not only because they were hung up, but because they were calling on a foreign
.31a God, saying "Have mercy on us." But I remembered days of festivity which we celebrated in Jerusalem before our captivity;

7.24-31 The text of ABarm is very much shorter here than that of Ceth, while P vacillates in its affinities, siding with Ceth in 7.24-26 but with ABarm thereafter. We have chosen to follow the longer text of Ceth. The parallel material in ABarm reads:
And Jeremiah wrote a letter to Jerusalem to Baruch and Abimelech before the whole people (concerning) the tribulations which had come upon them—how they had been taken away by the king of the Chaldeans, and how each man beheld his father bound, and each father his child subjected to punishment. But those who wanted to console the father covered his face lest he see his son being punished. And God covered you and Abimelech, lest you see us being punished; and when I remembered . . . (continues as in 7.31b)
For 7.24-26, where P sides with Ceth, the most significant variants are:
7.24 a letter to Baruch Ceth: to Baruch and Abimelech P (= ABarm)
7.24 my beloved son Ceth: beloved Baruch and Abimelech P
7.26 how his son is Ceth: his son P (= ABarm)—from here on, P sides with ABarm
In 7.29 God-ZAR is a cj of earlier editors (cf eth Sōr, Sorot): God SABAOTH C L

7.31b-8.3
καὶ μνησκόμενος ἐστέναζον, καὶ ἐπέστρεφον εἰς τὸν οἶκόν
μου ὀδυνώμενος
.32 καὶ κλαίων. Νῦν οὖν δεήθητι εἰς τὸν τόπον ὅπου εἶ, σὺ καὶ
Ἀβιμέλεχ, ὑπὲρ τοῦ λαοῦ τούτου, ὅπως εἰσακούσωσιν τῆς
φωνῆς μου καὶ
τῶν κριμάτων τοῦ στόματός μου καὶ ἐξέλθωμεν ἐντεῦθεν.
.33 Λέγω γάρ σοι ὅτι ὅλον τὸν χρόνον ὃν ἐποιήσαμεν ἐνταῦθα,
κατέχουσιν ἡμᾶς λέγοντες ὅτι,
Εἴπατε ἡμῖν ᾠδὴν ἐκ τῶν ᾠδῶν Σιών,
τὴν ᾠδὴν τοῦ θεοῦ ὑμῶν.
.34 Καὶ λέγομεν αὐτοῖς,
Πῶς ᾄσωμεν ὑμῖν
ἐπὶ γῆς ἀλλοτρίας ὄντες;
.35 Καὶ μετὰ ταῦτα ἔδησε τὴν ἐπιστολὴν εἰς τὸν τράχηλον τοῦ
ἀετοῦ Ἱερεμίας,
λέγων·
"Ἄπελθε ἐν εἰρήνῃ καὶ ἐπισκέψηται ἡμᾶς ἀμφοτέρους ὁ
κύριος.
.36 Καὶ ἐπετάσθη ὁ ἀετὸς, καὶ ἦλθεν εἰς Ἰερουσαλὴμ καὶ ἔδωκε τὴν
ἐπιστολὴν τῷ
Βαρούχ, καὶ λύσας ἀνέγνω καὶ κατεφίλησεν αὐτὴν καὶ ἔκλαυσε
ἀκούσας διὰ τὰς λύπας καὶ τὰς κακώσεις τοῦ λαοῦ.
.37 Ἱερεμίας δὲ ἄρας τὰ σῦκα διέδωκε τοῖς νοσοῦσι
τοῦ λαοῦ, καὶ ἔμεινε διδάσκων αὐτοὺς τοῦ ἀπέχεσθαι ἐκ τῶν
ἀλισγημάτων
τῶν ἐθνῶν τῆς Βαβυλῶνος.
8.1 Ἐγένετο δὲ ἡ ἡμέρα, ἐν ᾗ ἐξέφερε κύριος τὸν λαὸν ἐκ
Βαβυλῶνος.
.2 Καὶ εἶπεν ὁ κύριος πρὸς Ἱερεμίαν·
Ἀνάστηθι, σὺ καὶ ὁ λαός, καὶ δεῦτε ἐπὶ τὸν Ἰορδάνην,
καὶ ἐρεῖς
τῷ λαῷ·
Ὁ θέλων τὸν κύριον καταλειψάτω τὰ ἔργα τῆς Βαβυλῶνος.
.3 Καὶ τοὺς ἄρρενας τοὺς λαβόντας ἐξ αὐτῶν γυναῖκας, καὶ τὰς
γυναῖκας τὰς
λαβούσας ἐξ αὐτῶν ἄνδρας, διαπεράσωσιν οἱ ἀκούοντές σου,
καὶ ἆρον αὐτοὺς εἰς Ἱερουσαλήμ· τοὺς δὲ
μὴ ἀκούοντάς σου, μὴ εἰσαγάγῃς αὐτοὺς ἐκεῖ.

THE THINGS OMITTED FROM JEREMIAH

7.31b-8.3

7.31b and when I remembered, I groaned, and returned to my house wailing
.32 and weeping. Now, then, pray in the place where you are—you and Abimelech—for this people, that they may listen to my voice and
.33 to the decrees of my mouth, so that we may depart from here. For I tell you that the entire time that we have spent here they have kept us in subjection, saying:
>   Recite for us a song from the songs of Zion
>   [see Ps 136.3c/4]—the song of your God.
.34 And we reply to them:
>   How shall we sing for you
>   since we are in a foreign land? [Ps 136.4]
.35 And after this, Jeremiah tied the letter to the eagle's neck, saying:
>   Go in peace, and may the Lord watch over both of us.
.36 And the eagle took flight and came to Jerusalem and gave the letter to Baruch; and when he had untied it he read it and kissed it and wept when he heard about the distresses and afflictions of the people. But
.37 Jeremiah took the figs and distributed them to the sick among the people, and he kept teaching them to abstain from the pollutions of the gentiles of Babylon.

8.1 And the day came in which the Lord brought the people out of Babylon.
.2 And the Lord said to Jeremiah:
>   Rise up—you and the people—and come to the Jordan and say to the people:
>   Let anyone who desires the Lord forsake the works of Babylon.
.3 As for the men who took wives from them and the women who took husbands from them—those who listen to you shall cross over, and you take them into Jerusalem; but those who do not listen to you, do not lead them there.

7.31b and when I remembered—here the texts of Ceth and ABarm P become close again
.32 in the place where you are arm Ceth: om AB P
.32 that they may listen—mouth Ceth: that our (your, AB) prayer may be heard (+ before the Lord, arm) ABarm P
.37 pollutions AB (cf arm) P : works Ceth [see 8.2]

8.1 the Lord ABarm P : God Ceth
.2 the Lord AB Ceth : God arm P
.2 works AB (cf arm) P: + of the gentiles Ceth [see 7.37]

8.4-12

.4 Ἰερεμίας δὲ ἐλάλησεν πρὸς τὸν λαὸν τὰ ῥήματα τοῦτα· καὶ ἀναστάντες ἦλθον
.5 ἐπὶ τὸν Ἰορδάνην τοῦ περᾶσαι. Καὶ λέγων αὐτοῖς τὰ ῥήματα ἃ εἶπε κύριος
πρὸς αὐτόν, τὸ ἥμισυ τῶν γαμησάντων ἐξ αὐτῶν οὐκ ἠθέλησαν ἀκοῦσαι τοῦ Ἰερεμίου, ἀλλ' εἶπον πρὸς αἰτόν·
 Οὐ μὴ καταλείψωμεν τὰς γυναῖκας ἡμῶν εἰς τὸν αἰῶνα ἀλλ'
  ὑποστρέφωμεν αὐτὰς
 μεθ' ἡμῶν εἰς τὴν πόλιν ἡμῶν.
.6/ Ἐπέρασαν οὖν τὸν Ἰορδάνην καὶ ἦλθον εἰς Ἰερουσαλήμ. Καὶ
.7 ἔστη Ἰερεμίας καὶ
Βαροὺχ καὶ Ἀβιμέλεχ λέγοντες ὅτι,
 Πᾶς ἄνθρωπος κοινωνῶν Βαβυλωνίταις οὐ μὴ εἰσέλθῃ εἰς τὴν
  πόλιν ταύτην.
.8 Καὶ εἶπον πρὸς ἑαυτούς·
 Ἀναστάντες ὑποστρέψωμεν εἰς Βαβυλῶνα εἰς τὸν τόπον ἡμῶν·
.9 καὶ ἐπορεύθησαν. Ἐλθόντων δὲ αὐτῶν εἰς Βαβυλῶνα,
ἐξῆλθον οἱ Βαβυλωνῖται εἰς συνάντησιν αὐτῶν, λέγοντες·
 Οὐ μὴ εἰσέλθητε εἰς τὴν πόλιν ἡμῶν, ὅτι ἐμισήσατε ἡμᾶς,
  καὶ κρυφῇ ἐξήλθετε
 ἀφ' ἡμῶν· διὰ τοῦτο οὐκ εἰσελεύσεσθε πρὸς ἡμᾶς.
.10 Ορκῳ γὰρ ὡρκίσαμεν ἀλλήλους κατὰ τοῦ ὀνόματος τοῦ θεοῦ
 ἡμῶν,
 μήτε ὑμᾶς μήτε τέκνα ὑμῶν δέξασθαι, ἐπειδὴ κρυφῇ ἐξήλθετε
  ἀφ' ἡμῶν.
.11 Καὶ ἐπιγνόντες ὑπέστρεψαν καὶ ἦλθον εἰς τόπον ἔρημον
μακρόθεν τῆς Ἰερουσαλήμ, καὶ ᾠκοδόμησαν ἑαυτοῖς πόλιν, καὶ ἐπωνόμασαν τὸ ὄνομα
.12 αὐτῆς Σαμάρειαν. Ἀπέστειλε δὲ πρὸς αὐτοὺς Ἰερεμίας, λέγων·
 Μετανοήσατε· ἔρχεται γὰρ ἄγγελος τῆς δικαιοσύνης, καὶ
 εἰσάξει ὑμᾶς εἰς τὸν τόπον ὑμῶν τὸν ὑψηλόν.

8.4-12

8.4 And Jeremiah spoke these words to the people, and they arose and came
.5 to the Jordan to cross over. As he told them the words that the Lord had spoken to him, half of those who had taken spouses from them did not wish to listen to Jeremiah, but said to him:

We will never forsake our wives, but we will bring them back with us into our city.

.6/.7 So they crossed the Jordan and came to Jerusalem. And Jeremiah and Baruch and Abimelech stood up and said:

No man joined with Babylonians shall enter this city!

.8 And they said to one another:

Let us arise and return to Babylon to our place—

.9 And they departed. But while they were coming to Babylon, the Babylonians came out to meet them, saying:

You shall not enter our city, for you hated us and you left us
.10 secretly; therefore you cannot come in with us. For we have taken a solemn oath together in the name of our god to receive neither you nor your children, since you left us secretly.

.11 And when they heard this, they returned and came to a desert place some distance from Jerusalem and built a city for themselves and named it
.12 'SAMARIA.' And Jeremiah sent to them, saying:

Repent, for the angel of righteousness is coming and will lead you to your exalted place.

8.5 spouses from them—at this point, C leaves our text and continues with a variety of other materials related to the return from exile (Cyrus, Ezra, prayers, etc.)
.5 into our city eth : to Babylon ABarm P [see 8.8]
.8 to our place ABarm P : om eth [see 8.5]
.8 departed ABarm P : + and returned eth
.9 while they were coming to Babylon ABarm P : when the people of Babylon saw them eth
.9 in with us ABarm P : into our city eth
.12 place AB : + but they were not willing (did not listen, arm) arm P (cf eth?)

9.1 Ἔμειναν δὲ οἱ τοῦ Ἰερεμίου χαίροντες καὶ ἀναφέροντες
.2 θυσίας ὑπὲρ τοῦ λαοῦ ἐννέα ἡμέρας. Τῇ δὲ δεκάτῃ
.3 ἀνήνεγκεν Ἰερεμίας μόνος θυσίαν. Καὶ ηὔξατο εὐχὴν, λέγων·
Ἅγιος, ἅγιος, ἅγιος, τὸ θυμίαμα τῶν δένδρων τῶν ζώντων,
τὸ φῶς τὸ ἀληθινὸν τὸ φωτίζον με ἕως οὗ ἀναληφθῶ πρὸς σὲ·
.4 Περὶ τοῦ ἐλεώς σου, παρακαλῶ,
περὶ τῆς φωνῆς τῆς γλυκείας τῶν δύο Σεραφίμ,
παρακαλῶ,
περὶ ἄλλης εὐωδίας θυμιάματος.
.5 Καὶ ἡ μελέτη μου Μιχαὴλ ὁ ἀρχάγγελος τῆς δικαιοσύνης, ὁ ἀνοίγων
τὰς πύλας τοῖς δικαίοις, ἕως ἂν εἰσενέγκῃ τοὺς δικαίους.
.6 Παρακαλῶ σε, κύριε παντοκράτωρ πάσης κτίσεως, ὁ ἀγέννητος καὶ ἀπερινόητος,
ᾧ πᾶσα κρίσις κέκρυπται ἐν αὐτῷ πρὸ τοῦ ταῦτα γενέσθαι.
.7 Ταῦτα λέγοντος τοῦ Ἰερεμίου, καὶ ἱσταμένου ἐν τῷ θυσιαστηρίῳ
.8 μετὰ Βαροὺχ καὶ Ἀβιμέλεχ, ἐγένετο ὡς εἷς τῶν παραδιδόντων τὴν ψυχὴν αὐτοῦ. Καὶ
ἔμειναν Βαροὺχ καὶ Ἀβιμέλεχ κλαίοντες καὶ κράζοντες μεγάλῃ τῇ φωνῇ·
Οὐαὶ ἡμῶν ὅτι ὁ πατὴρ ἡμῶν Ἰερεμίας κατέλιπεν ἡμᾶς,
ὁ ἱερεὺς τοῦ θεοῦ καὶ ἀπῆλθεν.
.9 Ἤκουσε δὲ πᾶς ὁ λαὸς τοῦ κλαυθμοῦ αὐτῶν, καὶ ἔδραμον ἐπ' αὐτοὺς πάντες,
.10 καὶ εἶδον Ἰερεμίαν ἀνακείμενον χαμαὶ ὥσπερ τεθνηκότα. Καὶ διέρρηξαν τὰ ἱμάτια αὐτῶν, καὶ
.11 ἐπέθηκαν χοῦν ἐπὶ τὰς κεφαλὰς αὐτῶν, καὶ ἔκλαυσαν κλαυθμὸν πικρόν. Καὶ μετὰ ταῦτα ἡτοίμασαν
.12 ἑαυτοὺς ἵνα κηδεύσωσιν αὐτόν. Καὶ ἰδοὺ φωνὴ ἦλθε, λέγουσα·
Μὴ κηδεύετε τὸν ἔτι ζῶντα, ὅτι ἡ ψυχὴ αὐτοῦ εἰσέρχεται εἰς τὸ σῶμα αὐτοῦ πάλιν.
.13 Καὶ ἀκούσαντες τῆς φωνῆς, οὐκ ἐκήδευσαν αὐτόν, ἀλλ' ἔμειναν
περικύκλῳ τοῦ σκηνώματος αὐτοῦ ἡμέρας τρεῖς, λέγοντες ποιᾷ ὥρᾳ μέλλει ἀναστῆναι.
.14 Μετὰ δὲ τρεῖς ἡμέρας εἰσῆλθεν ἡ ψυχὴ αὐτοῦ εἰς τὸ σῶμα αὐτοῦ καὶ ἐπῆρε
τὴν φωνὴν αὐτοῦ ἐν μέσῳ πάντων καὶ εἶπε·
Δοξάσατε τὸν θεὸν ἐν μίᾳ φωνῇ, πάντες δοξάσατε τὸν θεὸν,
καὶ τὸν υἱὸν τοῦ θεοῦ τὸν ἐξυπνίζοντα ἡμᾶς, Ἰησοῦν χριστόν,
τὸ φῶς τῶν αἰώνων πάντων, ὁ ἄσβεστος λύχνος, ἡ ζωὴ τῆς πίστεως.

THE THINGS OMITTED FROM JEREMIAH

9.1-14

9.1 Now those who were with Jeremiah were rejoicing and offering
.2 sacrifices on behalf of the people for nine days. But on the tenth,
.3 Jeremiah alone offered sacrifice. And he prayed a prayer, saying:
    Holy, holy, holy, fragrant aroma of the living trees,
        true light that enlightens me until I ascend to you;
.4 For your mercy, I beg you—
    for the sweet voice of the two seraphim, I beg—
        for another fragrant aroma.
.5 And may Michael, archangel of righteousness, who opens the gates to the righteous, be my guardian (?) until he causes the righteous to enter.
.6 I beg you, almighty Lord of all creation, unbegotten and incomprehensible, in whom all judgment was hidden before these things came into existence.
.7 When Jeremiah has said this, and while he was standing in the altar-area with Baruch and Abimelech, he became as one whose soul has departed. And
.8 Baruch and Abimelech were weeping and crying out in a loud voice:
    Woe to us! For our father Jeremiah has left us—the priest of God has departed!
.9 And all the people heard their weeping and they all ran to them and saw
.10 Jeremiah lying on the ground as if dead. And they tore their garments and
.11 put dust on their heads and wept bitterly. And after this they prepared to
.12 bury him. And behold, there came a voice saying:
    Do not bury the one who yet lives, for his soul is returning to his body!
.13 And when they heard the voice they did not bury him, but stayed around his tabernacle for three days saying, "when will he arise?"
.14 And after three days his soul came back into his body and he raised his voice in the midst of them all and said:
    Glorify God with one voice! All of you glorify God and the son of God who awakens us—messiah Jesus—the light of all the ages, the inextinguishable lamp, the life of faith.

9.4 for your mercy I beg you arm P (cf eth) : om AB
.4 two AB P : holy arm : om eth
.4 seraphim ABarm P ; + and for the fragrant aroma of the cherubim eth
.4 for another fragrant aroma AB P : om arm eth (but see eth above)
.5 who opens the gates to the righteous P (cf eth) : om ABarm
.5 guardian (?) cf AB P : choir master (?) eth : arm lacks content
.6 in whom all judgment ABarm P (cf slav) : with whom the entire creation eth
.7 this ABarm P : + and when he had ended his prayer eth
.8 Woe to us P eth : om ABarm
.13 his tabernacle (=? body) AB P : his body arm : him eth [see 6.6f]
.13 wondering—arise cf ABarm P ; om eth
.14 with one voice P eth : om ABarm
.14 all of you glorify God and AB: Glorify God and all of you glorify the messiah eth: Glorify God and P: and arm
.14 messiah Jesus AB P hist : and will judge Jesus God's son eth : om arm

.15 Γίνεται δὲ μετὰ τοὺς καιροὺς τούτους ἄλλα ἔτη τετρακόσια
ἑβδομηκονταεπτὰ, καὶ
.16 ἔρχεται εἰς τὴν γῆν. καὶ τὸ δένδρον τῆς ζωῆς τὸ ἐν μέσῳ
τοῦ παραδείσου φυτευθὲν
ποιήσει πάντα τὰ δένδρα τὰ ἄκαρπα ποιῆσαι καρπόν,
καὶ αὐξηθήσονται, καὶ βλαστήσουσι.
.17 Καὶ τὰ δένδρα τὰ βεβλαστηκότα, καὶ μεγαλαυχοῦντα, καὶ
λέγοντα·
Ἐδώκαμεν τὸ τέλος ἡμῶν τῷ ἀέρι·
ποιήσει αὐτὰ ξηρανθῆναι μετὰ τοῦ ὕψους τῶν κλάδων αὐτῶν,
καὶ ποιήσει αὐτὰ κριθῆναι, τὸ δένδρον τὸ στηριχθέν.
.18 Καὶ τὸ κόκκινον ὡς ἔριον λευκὸν γενήσεται· ἡ χιὼν
μελανθήσεται,
τὰ γλυκέα ὕδατα ἁλμυρὰ γενήσονται καὶ τὰ ἁλμυρὰ γλυκέα
ἐν τῷ μεγάλῳ φωτὶ τῆς εὐφροσύνης τοῦ θεοῦ.
.19 Καὶ εὐλογήσει τὰς νήσους
τοῦ ποιῆσαι καρπὸν ἐν τῷ λόγῳ τοῦ στόματος τοῦ χριστοῦ
αὐτοῦ.
.20 Αὐτὸς γὰρ ἐλεύσεται,
καὶ ἐξελεύσεται καὶ ἐπιλέξεται ἑαυτῷ δώδεκα ἀποστόλους,
ἵνα εὐαγγελίζωνται ἐν τοῖς ἔθνεσιν·
ὃν ἐγὼ ἑώρακα κεκοσμημένον ὑπὸ τοῦ πατρὸς αὐτοῦ,
καὶ ἐρχόμενον εἰς τὸν κόσμον ἐπὶ τὸ ὄρος τῶν
ἐλαιῶν·
καὶ ἐμπλήσει τὰς πεινώσας ψυχάς.
.21 Ταῦτα λέγοντος τοῦ Ἰερεμίου περὶ τοῦ υἱοῦ τοῦ θεοῦ,
ὅτι ἔρχεται
εἰς τὸν κόσμον, ὠργίσθη ὁ λαὸς καὶ εἶπε·
Ταῦτα πάλιν ἐστὶ τὰ ῥήματα τὰ ὑπὸ Ἡσαΐου τοῦ υἱοῦ Ἀμὼς
εἰρημένα,
λέγοντος ὅτι,
Εἶδον τὸν θεόν, καὶ τὸν υἱὸν τοῦ θεοῦ.
.22 Δεῦτε οὖν, καὶ μὴ ἀποκτείνωμεν αὐτὸν τῷ ἐκείνου θανάτῳ,
ἀλλὰ λίθοις λιθοβολήσωμεν αὐτόν.

9.15-22

9.15 But after these times there shall be 477 years more and he comes to earth.
.16 And the tree of life planted in the midst of paradise
> will cause all the unfruitful trees to bear fruit,
>> and they will grow and sprout forth.
.17 And the trees that had sprouted and became haughty and said:
> "We have supplied our power (?) to the air,"
> he will cause them to wither, with the grandeur of their branches,
> and he will cause them to be judged—that firmly rooted tree!
.18 And what is crimson will become white as wool—the snow will be blackened—the sweet waters will become salty, and the salty sweet,
> in the intense light of the joy of God.
.19 And he will bless the isles
> so that they become fruitful by the word of the mouth of his messiah.
.20 For he shall come,
> and he will go out and choose for himself twelve apostles
>> to proclaim the news among the nations—
> he whom I have seen adorned by his father
>> and coming into the world on the Mount of Olives—
> and he shall fill the hungry souls.
.21 When Jeremiah was saying this concerning the son of God—that he is coming into the world—the people became very angry and said:
> This is a repetition of the words spoken by Isaiah son of Amos, when he said:
>> I saw God and the son of God.
.22 Come, then, and let us not kill him by the same sort of death with which we killed Isaiah, but let us stone him with stones.

9.15 477 years AB : 377 years P : 375 years more arm men-arm-b: 303 (var 330, 333) weeks of days eth : 275 years and some days men-arm-a
.16 trees ABarm P : + which are withered to come to him and he will cause them eth
.16 sprout forth ABarm P : + and their fruit will dwell with the angels eth
.17 we have supplied our power (?)—firmly rooted tree cf AB P : we caused our tops to reach the clouds we shall smite them and bring their lofty branches down he the everlasting tree arm : we will pay tribute to the air so that their roots will not wither like a plant whose roots had no depth eth
.18 the snow will be blackened ABarm P (cf men-arm) : om eth
.18 and the salty sweet eth : om ABarm P
.19 messiah ABarm men-arm : son P eth
.20 to proclaim—nations (gentiles) ABarm P : om eth
.22 not kill him—Isaiah AB (cf arm) P : do to him as we did to Isaiah but part of them said "No" eth
.22 stones AB (cf arm) P : + but Baruch and Abimelech cried out to them Do not kill him with this sort of death eth

9.23-32

.23 Ἐλυπήθησαν οὖν σφόδρα Βαροὺχ καὶ Ἀβιμέλεχ ὅτι ἤθελον
.24 ἀκοῦσαι πλήρης τὰ μυστήρια ἃ εἶδε. Λέγει δὲ αὐτοῖς Ἰερεμίας·
Σιωπήσατε καὶ μὴ κλαίετε·οὐ μὴ γάρ με ἀποκτείνωσιν
ἕως οὗ πάντα ὅσα εἶδον διηγήσωμαι ὑμῖν.
.25 Εἶπε δὲ αὐτοῖς·
Ἐνέγκατέ μοι λίθον ὧδε·
.26 Καὶ ἔστησεν αὐτὸν καὶ εἶπεν·
Τὸ φῶς τῶν αἰώνων,
ποίησον τὸν λίθον τοῦτον καθ' ὁμοιότητά μου γενέσθαι
ἕως οὗ πάντα ὅσα εἶδον διηγήσωμαι τῷ Βαροὺχ καὶ
τῷ Ἀβιμέλεχ.
.27 Τότε ὁ λίθος διὰ προστάγματος θεοῦ ἀνέλαβεν ὁμοιότητα τοῦ
Ἰερεμίου.
.28 Καὶ ἐλιθοβόλουν τὸν λίθον, νομίζοντες ὅτι Ἰερεμίας ἐστίν.
.29 Ὁ δὲ Ἰερεμίας πάντα παρέδωκε τὰ μυστήρια, ἃ εἶδε, τῷ
Βαροὺχ καὶ
τῷ Ἀβιμέλεχ, καὶ εἶθ' οὕτως ἔστη ἐν μέσῳ τοῦ λαοῦ,
.30 ἐκτελέσαι βουλόμενος τὴν οἰκονομίαν αὐτοῦ. Τότε ἐβόησε ὁ
λίθος, λέγων·
Ὦ μωροὶ υἱοὶ Ἰσραὴλ,
διὰ τί λιθοβολεῖτέ με, νομίζοντες ὅτι ἐγὼ Ἰερεμίας;
Ἰδοὺ Ἰερεμίας ἐν μέσῳ ὑμῶν ἵσταται.
.31 Ὡς δὲ εἶδον αὐτόν, εὐθέως ἔδραμον πρὸς αὐτὸν μετὰ πολλῶν
λίθων,
καὶ ἐπληρώθη αὐτοῦ οἰκονομία.
.32 Καὶ ἐλθόντες Βαροὺχ καὶ Ἀβιμέλεχ, ἔθαψαν αὐτὸν, καὶ
λαβόντες τὸν λίθον ἔθηκαν ἐπὶ τὸ μνῆμα αὐτοῦ, ἐπιγράψαντες
ἐν αὐτῷ οὕτως·
Οὗτός ἐστιν ὁ λίθος ὁ βοηθὸς τοῦ Ἰερεμίου.

9.23-32

9.23 And Baruch and Abimelech were greatly grieved because they wanted
.24 to hear in full the mysteries that he had seen. But Jeremiah said to them:
Be silent and weep not, for they cannot kill me
until I describe for you everything I saw.
.25 And he said to them:
Bring a stone here to me.
.26 And he set it up and said:
Light of the ages,
make this stone to become like me in appearance,
until I have described to Baruch and Abimelech everything I saw.
.27 Then the stone, by God's command, took on the appearance of Jeremiah.
.28 And they were stoning the stone, supposing that it was Jeremiah!
.29 But Jeremiah delivered to Baruch and to Abimelech all the mysteries he had seen, and forthwith he stood in the midst of the people desiring to
.30 complete his ministry. Then the stone cried out, saying:
O foolish children of Israel,
why do you stone me, supposing that I am Jeremiah?
Behold, Jeremiah is standing in your midst!
.31 And when they saw him, immediately they rushed upon him with many stones, and his ministry was fulfilled.
.32 And when Baruch and Abimelech came, they buried him, and taking the stone they placed it on his tomb and inscribed it thus:
This is the stone that was the ally of Jeremiah.

9.23 grieved arm P eth men-arm hist : + at this madness AB
.26 And H (cf ABarm) : And when they brought (it) P WS (cf O) : And they brought him a stone eth (cf men-arm hist)
.26 me ABarm P men-arm : a man eth
.27 by God's command ABarm P men-arm hist : om eth
.29 all AB eth men-arm : om arm P
.31 fulfilled AB (cf arm eth: + delivering his worthy and holy soul into the hands of the living God on the first of the month of May P (cf men-arm)
.32 tomb ABarm P: + and set it up as a door eth (cf men-arm-b and hist, as a witness/memorial)
.32 This ABarm P men-arm hist: Behold this eth
subscription And the rest of the words of Jeremiah and all his mighty work (the history of this writing of Paraleipomena, arm), are they not written in the letter of Baruch (+ glory be to Christ forever, Amen; arm) ABarm: And all power to Christ Jesus our Lord to whom be glory and might forever and ever, amen P (= Oxford Bodl. B. 240.2)